WHAT OTHERS ARE SAYING
ABOUT *THE MASQUERADE*

WE LIVE IN an age of deception. Who can be deceived? The simple. The very elect. Evil men and seducers. We deceive ourselves. Everyone can be deceived, including you and me.

Deceivers drift in and out of ministries, claiming to have special revelations from God. They undermine spiritual authority and are accountable to no one but themselves. Their manipulative charm and charismatic manifestations are not accompanied by the Fruit of the Spirit. And many ministries have been decimated by deceivers. Be alert!

In *The Masquerade*, Donna Sparks masterfully exposes deception and how it lures someone into its web of deceit. Deception occurs in every area of life whether ethics, philosophy, morality, religion, or sexuality. But be encouraged, because the king of counterfeits, Satan, has been defeated by the Light of the world, Jesus Christ.

The Masquerade will enable your ministry to exercise greater discernment.

—Terry G. Bailey, District Superintendent
Tennessee Assemblies of God Ministry Network

THE MASQUERADE

DECEPTION IN THE LAST DAYS

Donna Sparks

BRIDGE LOGOS

Newberry, FL 32669

Bridge-Logos
Newberry, FL 32669

The Masquerade: Deception in the Last Days
by Donna Sparks

Printed in the United States of America.

Library of Congress Catalog Card Number: 2020940387

International Standard Book Number: 978-1-61036-248-1

Cover/Interior design by Kent Jensen | knail.com

Literary Agent and Editor,
L. Edward Hazelbaker
E-mail: l.edward@thewornkeyboard.com

DEDICATION

. . . .

TO CAROL BROWN and my Northside Assembly of God Bible study ladies, who have read and shared my previous books. You ladies inspire me to keep writing, and I love you all, my sweet sisters!

To my ministry partner, Brenda Overton, who travels with me, encourages me, and puts up with me.

Also, to my *jail ladies*, who—by their testimonies—inspire me to keep sharing the gospel with those who are bound by Satan's chains of deception.

FOREWORD

MOST PEOPLE KNOW the June 1944 invasion of Normandy, the largest seaborne assault in history, as "D-Day." It was an offensive that changed the tide of World War II and led to the Allied victory over the Nazis. What many people do not realize, however, was that the Normandy landings were successful, in large part, due to a massive deception.

The Allied forces used double agents, mock radio messages, and visual tricks to convince Hitler that attacks were coming elsewhere at a later date. Because of that, he failed to send reinforcements and was taken by surprise.

Deception and trickery are so common in war that the *ruse de guerre*—or ruse of *war*—is studied by strategists and represents an entire category of military tactics. These methods are not new either. The Greeks used deception against Troy in the famous tale of the Trojan Horse. Even the ancient Chinese military book, *The Art of War*, emphasizes deception as one of the most important tools in the strategist's arsenal.

But long before Hitler, the Greeks, or even the Ancient Chinese, the great enemy of humanity has been using deception as his most potent weapon against us. As far back as the Garden of Eden, the serpent *"deceived Eve by his cunning"* (2 Corinthians 11:3 ESV). And he is still using the same tricks on the unwitting world to this day.

Unregenerate man has no answer for the wiles of the devil. Without spiritual armor—and ignorant of the imminent danger—humanity walks blindly through a deep spiritual jungle, where hideous, hungry beasts prey on the unwitting (1 Peter 5:8). But we, God's Children, have been equipped with the tools and wisdom to resist the devil.

Paul told the Corinthians to forgive and restore a person there *"lest Satan should get an advantage of us: for we are not ignorant of his devices"* (2 Corinthians 2:11 NKJV). There is a relationship between *ignorance* and *advantage*. The devil has the upper hand against those who are oblivious to his schemes. But God's Word exposes the devil's playbook and gives us the high ground.

I believe in this hour, perhaps more than ever before, God is calling His people to be sober and alert. We are living at a time when deception abounds, and as we draw nearer to the end of the age, we are promised that it will only increase (Matthew 24:24, 1 Timothy 4:1, 2 Timothy 4:3-4).

God is calling for *watchmen on the wall*, who will see the enemy coming and sound the alarm. I believe Donna Sparks is one of those watchers. In *The Masquerade*, Donna addresses specific and important issues that threaten the Church today—cessationism, division, spiritual counterfeits, identity crisis, and more.

Donna's boldness and clarity are exactly what we need today. The book you hold in your hands will not only open your eyes—will not only give you the tactical advantage over the enemy in your life—I believe it will equip you, too, to be a watchman on the wall.

—Daniel Kolenda, Evangelist
President/CEO, Christ for All Nations

TABLE OF CONTENTS

INTRODUCTION

AN "AGENDA" IS a list, plan, or outline of things to be done. The usage note on the website, Dictionary.com, says, "Agenda, 'things to be done,' is the plural of the Latin gerund *agendum* and is used today in the sense 'a plan or list of matters to be acted upon.'"[1]

Stated or unstated—and written or unwritten—agendas can be seen all around us. Clearly, politicians have agendas. Teachers have agendas. News Media personalities have agendas (and oh boy, do they go beyond reporting the news!). Agendas are everywhere. And hopefully you and I have great agendas as we plan to accomplish a lot for God.

Agendas are developed all the time to help people accomplish *goals.* And goals are basically the things people pursue—what they are trying to accomplish.

Motive is another good word for you to think about as you start reading this book. Motive has to do with incentives. Our motives are determined by what we believe we have to gain by reaching our Goals. A good way to understand motives is to think about how we are *motivated* to pursue our goals—how reaching those goals is going to benefit us.

So basically, *agendas* contain our plans for accomplishing our goals. And the pleasure and satisfaction we receive by reaching our goals drive our *motives.* Does that make sense? Stated another way, a goal is *what* I want to reach. A motive is *why* I want to reach it. And an agenda is *how* I plan to go about reaching it.

---

1   https://www.dictionary.com/browse/agenda

The *whats, whys,* and *hows* are behind all our actions, but it is definitely the *hows*—the agendas—that are most often seen first. And by examining, recognizing, and identifying agendas we begin to gain insight into the others.

We see people working their agendas every day. Agendas can be seen in something as simple as advertising and sales in the business world. And they can be seen in something as positive as the strategies and work of Christian organizations as they go about fulfilling the Great Commission.

Agendas, goals, and motives are not dirty words. But just as they can be revealed in something as valuable and joyful as bringing the lost to Christ and setting the captives free, they can also be associated with deception and destruction. And that should come across to you in this book.

While I don't write directly about agendas, goals, and motives in great detail, hopefully by reading this book you will be encouraged to examine and recognize how these things exist in physical and spiritual interactions both inside and outside churches. Because there is value in knowing how they reveal to us who people really are and why they do what they do.

But there's more.

All three of these things—agendas, goals, and motives—are revealed in the destructive activities of our enemy, Satan. And they are found in the activities of others who either wittingly or unwittingly yield themselves to Satan's deceptions as they go about attempting to undermine and destroy God's plans.

Just as God has an agenda for our good, the devil has an agenda for our destruction. And Satan is motivated by the pleasure and satisfaction he gains by seeing God's work hindered, His Creation ruined, and people's lives shattered. And those *are* Satan's goals.

But knowing that, alone, will not deliver us from the enemy's devices. We must allow the Holy Spirit to impart knowledge to us so we will recognize deception everywhere it exists. But we also must allow the Holy Spirit to give us wisdom for dealing with deception in a way that brings life to us and glory to God.

And we must allow the Holy Spirit to not only enable us to overcome Satan's deceptions but also empower us to deliver others from his deceptive work.

Multitudes of people continually live in deception. They are living their lives in darkness without even realizing it. They need Jesus—the only Light that will illuminate the deception and drive it away from them.

Deception is rampant in the world. Lies are masquerading as truth today like at no other time in such a worldwide fashion. And every day, masses of people are satisfied and fooled by only what they see on the surface of the deceptive masks worn by those lies instead of looking behind them to see the evil hiding and lurking there ready to wreck their lives and possibly consume them.

It is our duty as Christians to not only avoid and reject deception but also help others to do the same thing. We need to remove the masks covering up Satan's goals, motives, and agendas.

But as you begin reading, I want to stress to you that we can't do that by merely placing the blame for everything bad in the world at Satan's feet. For people are more than just a little prone to give him a lot of very fertile soil in which to plant his seeds of deception.

In fact, people are often eager to even help Satan plant those destructive seeds. And after they have planted them in their own back yards, they're all too happy to help their neighbors plant seeds on their property too.

Satan definitely goes about masquerading as an angel of light as he spreads and supports deception among us. But people themselves not only accept the devil's masquerade but also go about inventing and throwing masquerade parties of their own as they pursue their own goals and develop their own agendas.

Often in his work of promoting deception, all Satan has to do is just support and cheer on people's own efforts to deny and cover up the truth. So, many times you'll find the masked enemy of our souls merely standing along the wall, just inside the door at their parties, simply handing out the party favors to those who were invited to attend.

With this book I am attempting to get people to look behind the masks of deception no matter who or what is wearing them. And for those of you who already recognize the masks and know what's under them, I hope to encourage you and equip you to help others understand and overcome deception. As Christians answering God's call to action, that is our work.

It's time to interrupt the agendas of all who spread deception. It's time to bring their masquerade to an end.

—Donna

CHAPTER 1

SOUND
THE ALARM

I WAS ACTUALLY sitting in my basement waiting for a tornado to hit our area—or hopefully dissipate and go away—as I began to think about the subject of this chapter. It's that time of year here in Tennessee, and tornado watches and warnings are not uncommon. I was thinking about how fortunate we are to have early-warning systems to alert us to take cover when danger is headed our way.

As I pondered that, I began to think about all the meteorologists and scientists who have studied and worked for years to bring about the technology that provides advance-warning services to us. Those meteorologists and scientists began working on those services for a single purpose—to warn others of imminent danger or possible death.

After all that work, and knowing the benefits of it, would we not find it foolish in this day and age if people were protesting or trying to get the meteorologists to shut up and quit sharing information that could save lives?

Imagine people participating in activities outside—doing things they really enjoy—and the tornado sirens start to blow. Would it be reasonable for them to get upset with the early-warning system and curse the work of its developers and those who maintain and employ the system because their plans and activities have been interrupted?

Can you imagine people telling you they have never personally seen a tornado, so they doubt they're real? Or perhaps they would tell you they refuse to pay attention to the warnings because the very thought of tornadoes coming their way *offends* them. Or perhaps they would say since they have heard the sirens blowing so many times without a tornado ever appearing, they are sure one could never affect *them*.

Imagine people in their anger lashing out at those attempting to save their lives by telling them, "Stop bothering us, we don't believe in tornadoes."

Wouldn't that be foolish?

And with all we know today, wouldn't it be unreasonable to think that officials should stop sounding the alarms because people refuse to listen to the warnings and take them seriously? And wouldn't it be ludicrous to rally against meteorologists and ask the media or government to silence them?

Wouldn't it be foolish for people to protest against others who are actually trying to save their lives?

Yet, people are often guilty of reacting in similar ways when it comes to God's efforts to save their souls and warn them of danger. Too often they do all they can to shut their ears, deny truth, and refuse to accept the warnings and messages meant to save and protect them. They even oppose—and some even openly campaign against—anyone who proclaims to them God's warnings.

As Christians, perhaps we should see ourselves as part of God's early-warning system. Because warning others is exactly part of what we should be doing if we are following Christ in fulfilling the Great Commission.

As followers of Jesus, we believe in trying to rescue those who are facing imminent danger. We understand and want to share with them what wonderful happiness, joy, and peace is available to those who avoid danger by entering into and finding safety in a relationship with Christ.

We desire to share the same hope and safety we have found!

But many in the world of unbelievers see us as meddlers or bigots. They reject our message. Many don't believe in God or the Holy Bible. And many have chosen to believe in their own kind of god and knowingly reject God's truth. But of course their choices have not affected God or His message. So Christians who honor the truth continue to spread God's messages of warnings and salvation.

Tornadoes will not cease to exist because people don't believe in them. And if in our own opinion we were to believe an F5 tornado is nothing more than a strong wind that can do no lasting harm, that's certainly not going to make it less powerful.

Similarly, not believing in God will not make Him cease to exist. And anyone thinking his or her opinion takes precedence over what the Bible actually reveals about God and His message to us will never affect the authority and power of the Word of God.

People who think their views and opinions are higher than God's are deceiving themselves.

How silly it would be to disable all tornado sirens because a few people have never experienced a tornado, don't believe in tornadoes, or have no respect for them. And how utterly ludicrous it would be for the Church to stop sharing God's warnings of the danger of ignoring, rejecting, or twisting the Truth.

A couple of years ago a particular phrase became popular and began to grace T-shirts, baseball caps, keychains, and other items. And it was not surprising to hear people repeat it: "It's all relative." I searched for this phrase on the internet to clear up my own understanding of the actual sentiment behind it.

The consensus of most sources explained it to mean that the world is in the *eye of the beholder*. In other words, what things *are* depends on how people look at them. That is, everyone looks at things from a different perspective, and each person's opinion or view about something defines it.

So following that idea, the way we see an issue or what we believe about it will affect how it becomes either serious or frivolous, real or fake, or true or false for us. So in that way of thinking, truth simply depends on our own individual perspectives.

I definitely disagree with that notion and recognize it as a deceptive attack on God's truth.

The truth contained in the Word of God is not relative to our own private feelings and interpretations.[2] Nor is it dictated by whether or not we like what the Bible says. The Word of God is just that; it is what God says—God's word to us—and our individual *perspective* on it is irrelevant in any attempt to change what God says.

Regardless of how anyone wants to see it, the Bible is still the Word of God, and **its truth does not change**.

---

2   2 Peter 1:20.

God inspired the assembly of the Bible, and He knows what He intends to do with it.[3] The Holy Spirit inspired the writers of the Bible to write what they did.[4] But further, the Holy Spirit not only inspired the writing of the Bible, He continues to work today to reveal the Bible's truths to us.[5]

We must never allow ourselves to yield to any deception that moves us away from trusting God's Word toward trusting man's changing views. Man's changing thoughts about things will never change what God thinks. God never changes, and anyone's attempt to twist God's words to suit personal views is a futile exercise.

Truth is truth, but too many people have stopped believing it, and too many Christians have stopped *speaking* it. In this book I do my best to not only expose deceptions and falsehoods but also highlight the need for all believers to speak out truth against deception and expose how falsehoods are used to undermine God's work in us and in the world.

I feel called to do this, and I believe God is calling all of us to oppose deception and warn others of its destructive nature everywhere it exists.

We must call out deceptive teachings and call out the enemy of our souls, who fosters, stirs up, supports, encourages, and uses deception in his attempts to hinder God's work and destroy His

3 "All Scripture is inspired by God and is useful to teach us what is true and to make us realize what is wrong in our lives. It corrects us when we are wrong and teaches us to do what is right. God uses it to prepare and equip his people to do every good work" (2 Timothy 3:16-17).

4 "Above all, you must realize that no prophecy in Scripture ever came from the prophet's own understanding or from human initiative. No, those prophets were moved by the Holy Spirit, and they spoke from God" (2 Peter 1:20-21).

5 "But when the Father sends the Advocate as my representative—that is, the Holy Spirit—he will teach you everything and will remind you of everything I have told you" (John 14:26). "But when the Spirit of truth comes, he will guide you into all truth" (John 16:13a).

plans. But for us to battle against deception we must have a firm grip on how to separate truth from fiction.

As the father of lies,[6] Satan constantly opposes, twists, and misrepresents the truth. And in their own quest for superiority and search for self-gratification, people all too often accept the enemy's lies and start making up their own. And with that, they adopt deceptive ways, and many of them become obedient soldiers in the enemy's army that spreads deception to others.

There is a great need for people of faith to confront the devil's army of deception and sound the alarm to warn others of danger as it approaches them. We must do it, and it will be done by directly opposing and unmasking deception so people will see and realize the threat it poses to them.

The Holy Spirit leads the followers of Jesus in that work. But the Holy Spirit will not be able to work through us as individual believers to take the deceptive masks off of Satan's forces without our cooperation.

We must *allow* the Holy Spirit to work through us! We must seek His empowerment!

But we must also *know* our enemy. We will be ill-suited to raise the flag of truth in victory over Satan's soldiers of deception until we understand the perverted ways in which they operate. And God will give us that understanding if we want it.

Just as so many people have dedicated themselves to studying the nature and development of tornadoes to establish an effective early-warning system that saves lives today, we must dedicate ourselves to studying the nature and development of deception. And that starts with studying the Bible and allowing the Holy Spirit to guide us in our own *spiritual* development.

Then, with the knowledge we need to identify deception, with the enablement of the Holy Spirit, and with the truth of

---

6   John 8:44.

God's Word in our hand to confront falsehoods, we are prepared to sound the alarm to warn others of approaching danger. And we must do that whether or not people accept the warnings.[7]

In our preparation to deal with deception, let's pause to think about the Church's actual responsibility to expose and defeat it. Because when looking for something or someone to blame for people living in deception, we must admit—if we are willing to be completely honest—that a lot of people naming the name of Christ over many centuries have contributed (and still contribute) to confusion with their own inabilities to separate truth from fiction.

And as we point out people's fault for opposing and rejecting truth—we must realize that Christians, themselves, are also too often at fault for adding to the confusion by remaining silent and failing to warn others of the consequences of ignoring or violating the truth.

As I consider reasons why many Christians continue to be silent instead of speaking out against lies, deception, and ungodly views and behavior, I can't keep from wondering if it's partly because Christians in our society have become too complacent and soft. I wonder if over the years all too many have come to think the cost of speaking out is too high a price to pay.

Perhaps in our day and age we're more prone to want to let people go their own ways—even if that means they are eternally lost—as long as it doesn't affect the world around us. And perhaps it just hurts our feelings too much for people to call us names— names like holy roller, Bible thumper, prude, homophobe, racist, hate monger, or bigot—when we call out their lies.

---

7   Ezekiel 33:1-9.

As for those of us who do regularly speak the truth to others, many of us have been ridiculed, teased, laughed at, or attacked. And that has caused some Christians to stop speaking out. It's not easy to share the gospel when people refuse to hear it. And it's worse when we are mistreated for doing it. But that doesn't relieve us of our obligation to deliver the truth to others.

Experiencing the pain of rejection is real, and it's no fun. But we need to rise up against any pain inflicted upon us by others, pray for boldness, and continue to speak out. Yes, when we speak the truth we can be assured there will be those who oppose us for it. But we should not be surprised by that. The Bible tells us we will be persecuted for following and representing Christ.

> *Yes, and all who desire to live godly in Christ Jesus will suffer persecution.* (2 Timothy 3:12 NKJV)

> *If the world hates you, remember that it hated me first. The world would love you as one of its own if you belonged to it, but you are no longer part of the world. I chose you to come out of the world, so it hates you.* (John 15:18-19)[8]

> *God blesses you when people mock you and persecute you and lie about you and say all sorts of evil things against you because you are my followers.* (Matthew 5:11)

Just knowing these things, though, doesn't make it a whole lot easier to handle persecution when it comes our way, especially when persecution goes beyond verbal attacks to physical mistreatment. But perhaps we should remind ourselves that Christians in some parts of the world are still being killed for sharing the gospel. That should make Christians who have stopped speaking out for Christ because of name calling a bit ashamed.

---

8   Unless otherwise indicated, all Scripture quotations are taken from the New Living Translation of the Bible.

We must continue telling it like it is regardless of hurt feelings, disappointment, and rejection. We absolutely must not value our feelings over the importance of God's work.

Just as the officials in charge of warning people of approaching storms continue their work regardless of how people feel about it, we must continue to sound the alarm to warn people about the destructive lies and deceptions that the enemies of God are bringing against them regardless of any discomfort we may feel by doing it.

Sadly, we can no longer say we Americans live in a Christian nation. But now is no time for any disappointment over that to stop us from proclaiming the truth. Now is no time for the Church's warning sirens to become rusty and seize up.

Pride and ungodliness have invaded our society. And it's sad but true that entire churches and church organizations are struggling today to keep pride and ungodliness from taking them over, and some of them are losing. But that's even more reason for us, who are called to bring Christ's light to the world, to shine all the more brightly.

I can't help but be reminded of pictures I have seen of people in developing nations attending church as they stood in knee-deep flood waters. Many of us would stay home, and leaders would even cancel church, if we merely found that the air conditioning in the building had stopped working.

In too many places in our society, Christianity has turned into just another religion. And for many who attend church today, maintaining some form of godly devotion has become more about pursuing validation for ungodly views, comfort, and what else can be gained to satisfy them instead of being about worshiping God, leading others to Jesus, and sounding the alarm to warn people about the dangers of deceptions and lies.

We must change that.

I was ministering in a church recently where I overheard an elderly gentleman talking about how bad this world had become. He said he had just shut himself off from the world and was simply waiting for Jesus to come back or take him home, because it was pointless to "try anymore."

I must admit, it would be easy to feel that way if we were to give in to discouragement over the world's condition and what we've seen Satan accomplish by deceiving people—especially when that has happened with friends and family.

But that man's attitude is not acceptable.

Regardless of how bad we feel things are, and no matter how hopeless things may seem, we must keep sounding the alarm. Perhaps one lost soul will hear and respond to the warning in time to find shelter in the arms of Christ before slipping into eternity. Only one response like that will be a satisfying reward for all the many times we have sounded the alarm before without anyone responding.

And it will be well worth years of facing discomfort or persecution for proclaiming the gospel when we see any soul delivered from being imprisoned behind bars of deception. We must set off the warning siren and proclaim the One who frees the captives and rescues the perishing. We must do what we can, and let God do what we *can't*.

The importance and necessity of sounding the alarm is set clearly in Scripture in Christ's own words.

> *Behold, I am coming quickly, and My reward is with Me, to render to every man according to what he has done.*
> (Revelation 22:12 NASB)

The message of the Bible is clear; Jesus is coming soon, and everyone will answer to Him.

It's going to happen, and the Bible couldn't be clearer about it. Sound the alarm! People must know even if they don't want to hear it.

Point people to Scripture to find out more about Christ's return and other things surrounding what to expect in the last days. Proclaim the truth and lead people to know more about avoiding deception as the world approaches judgment.

We must sound the alarm and point people to the Word of God if we're going to draw them out of living in deception. The truth is revealed in Scripture. If people now living in deception want to know the truth, they will find it in the Bible.

And when it comes to understanding the truths contained in the Scriptures, people don't need an advanced degree in theology to learn what the Bible reveals about the main issues of life, truth, and deception. We can trust the Holy Spirit to give people the necessary understanding they need if they will actually read the Bible and apply themselves to the Holy Spirit's guidance. And that's part of our message.

In fact, although I'm in favor of lifelong Bible study and the pursuit of theological understanding, there are many well-educated theologians in the world whose *theology* itself has become twisted into pretzels of deception because their focus has switched from knowing God to developing and promoting beliefs that satisfy their own interests and curiosities. And we must make warning people of their deceptive teachings part of the alarm we sound.

People need to know this! People need to know the truth! And we must proclaim it. Be bold to declare all the truth found in the Bible. Reveal to others the dangers that lie beneath the masks of deception worn by those who may speak in glowing terms about God but oppose Christ's lordship over them.

Satan has been promoting lies and twisting the truth for a very long time. He's good at it, and multitudes have been swept up in his twisted, deceptive ways. But as long as there are Christians willing to stand up, proclaim the truth, and confront lies head on, there is hope for those now living in deception.

No name calling, no intimidation, and no persecution will cause the Lord's early-warning system to go silent as long as the Holy Spirit gives wisdom, power, and boldness to those of us willing to sound the alarm and faithfully stand before the enemy to speak God's truths against Satan's and the world's lying deceptions.

Yes, deception is strong. And yes, confronting it may not be pleasant at times. Like Goliath standing before the armies of the Children of Israel, deception can stand before us, make its boasts, and attempt to intimidate us. And the giant's name calling alone may be enough to intimidate and dissuade many people from going into battle with him.

But not all will cower in fear of the enemy. For we know the enemy's boasts and threats are, themselves, an exercise of deception. Like David standing before Goliath, people of faith will reject fear that paralyzes others and enter the battle against deception and lies.

They will not be stopped. They will declare and carry God's truth into battle—sounding the alarm for others to hear as they go—and their victory will be the Lord's.

David replied to [the giant, Goliath], "You come to me with sword, spear, and javelin, but I come to you in the name of the LORD of Heaven's Armies—the God of the armies of Israel, whom you have defied. Today the LORD will conquer you, and I will kill you and cut off your head. And . . . the whole world will know that there is a God in Israel! And everyone assembled here will know that the LORD *rescues his people, but not with sword and spear. This is the* LORD's *battle, and he will give you to us!"*

. . .

So David triumphed over the Philistine with only a sling and a stone, for he had no sword. Then David ran over and pulled Goliath's sword from its sheath. David used it to kill him and cut off his head. (1 Samuel 17:45-51b)

For I am not ashamed of this Good News about Christ. It is the power of God at work, saving everyone who believes—the Jew first and also the Gentile. (Romans 1:16)

But [Paul] said, "Why all this weeping? You are breaking my heart! I am ready not only to be jailed at Jerusalem but even to die for the sake of the Lord Jesus." (Acts 21:13)

For God has not given us a spirit of fear and timidity, but of power, love, and self-discipline. (2 Timothy 1:7)

DISCUSSION QUESTIONS

1. What fears or concerns do you have when it comes to sharing your faith with unbelievers?

2. Think about how you answered the previous question. What advice would you give to friends if they told you they were afraid to share their faith?

---

3. We often have good advice to share with others, but we rarely want to listen to our own advice. Why do you think we do that?

---

4. 2 Timothy 1:7 tells us that God has not given us a spirit of fear and timidity. Since we know fear is not from God, where do you think your fears come from, and why?

---

5. When we read the rest of 2 Timothy 1:7, we see that in the place of fear God has given us power, love, and self-discipline. These three things empower us to share our faith. In light of this, what could you do to be more vocal in sharing the Gospel?

_____

_____

_____

_____

_____

_____

6. According to John 8:31-32, why is it so important to hold fast to the teachings of Jesus and to know the truth?

_____

_____

_____

_____

_____

_____

CHAPTER 2

THE IDENTITY CRISIS

MOST OF US have heard people say they were going through an *identity crisis*. In my younger years when a person said he or she was going through an identity crisis, it typically meant the individual could be unsure about something as insignificant as a hairstyle change. Or it could have been something more significant, like a career choice.

But in today's society it can have a much more serious meaning. Never has a generation been more confused about its identity. In my opinion, we are living in one of the most—if not *the most*—severe ages of deception of all times. And I'm afraid that *identity* has become a serious topic that we as Christians too often shy away from. I'll admit that I, myself, have sidestepped the topic a few times.

Until . . .

A recent experience shook me to my core. I believe God was speaking to me personally through it and attempting to get me re-centered and back in alignment with the Holy Bible. And it most definitely worked.

I have shared many times in my books, website, and social media posts about my jail and prison ministry. I speak to many female inmates on a weekly basis, and I praise God for all of the wonderful things He has done and continues to do through this ministry. I do my very best to give prisoners the truth with love and compassion.

Not long ago as I was ministering in the local jail, a precious young lady gave her heart to Christ. We will call her *Angel* (not her real name) to honor her privacy.

After her salvation, Angel became hungry for more of God, and it was obvious the Lord had impacted her life in a powerful way. I could sense a strong call to ministry on her life, and she wanted everything God had to offer her.

Angel called me after she was released from jail. She was so excited as we talked about her long drive home with her father! She related to me how she had told him everything she learned in the jail services. She talked about the Bible lessons I had shared with them and how my testimony had inspired her to follow Jesus. I was so thrilled to hear the excitement in her voice.

But it kept getting better.

She said, "Miss Donna, when I got home I sat down with my family and read the Bible to them! But that's not all. I prayed with them, and they accepted Christ as their Savior."

I almost shouted right then and there!

She continued, "And Miss Donna, we have found a wonderful church just a few miles from our house. We are all going this Sunday!"

I was overjoyed! She shared the name of the church with me, and I told her I would give the pastor a call on Monday. When I called him, he shared with me that she and her parents *did* go to church that Sunday. And he told me their church had just started a new program for former addicts and those fighting addictions. He also shared with me his plans to get Angel involved.

And he did just that!

Angel soon called me back bursting with excitement as she told me how the pastor was getting her planted in several areas of ministry. She seemed so excited to be involved and to be able to see God moving in her life. I was overjoyed to hear such wonderful news. I could not have been happier for her.

But as time continued on, Angel became silent.

Then after some time her pastor emailed me to tell me that Angel was in a romantic relationship with another female and was no longer attending the church. He had recently preached a message in which he shared Scriptures on sin—including the sin of homosexuality. Angel and her significant other got out of their seats and left the service.

The pastor told me he tried to reach out to her many times since then, but to no avail.

My heart sank. "How could she not have known?" I thought.

I then started asking myself more questions.

"Did I preach on it in the jail?" I questioned. "Did I sweep over the issue assuming they all *knew* what sin was? After all, I've heard so many people say, 'Everyone understands what sin is. You don't have to point it out to them. It's not *your* job to judge.' Have I accepted that as truth? When did I start believing that sharing the truth was judging?"

I tried to recall at least one time when Angel was sitting in a jail church service when I shared the truth about homosexual lifestyles being sinful. I couldn't remember one, and I planned to contact Angel as soon as I could muster up the courage to speak to her about it.

That moment didn't come, though, before she contacted me on Facebook. I was amazed to see how much she resembled a man in her profile picture. She contacted me to see if I would be willing to help her with a Christian ministry Facebook page she had started to help women and children.

When I checked out the page, I noticed many other members who were also in lesbian relationships. And they were using a *Christian title* on the page!

I was reeling from shock, especially when I saw that she had linked the page to my personal website!

"Lord, what have I done?" I whispered in desperation. I prayed and asked the Holy Spirit to help me.

Angel did not want to speak to me over the phone, so I had to send her a typed response. It went like this:

> Angel, I want you to know first and foremost that I love you, and I would never ever want to hurt you. But because I love you and care about you, I must tell you the truth. You cannot live a homosexual lifestyle and be a Christian. Homosexuality is a sin. When we accept Christ as our Savior we must turn from our sins and follow Him.

> I feel I have failed you by allowing you to leave the jail believing this type of lifestyle is acceptable. It is not. If I didn't care about you I wouldn't be telling you this. But *I do care*, and I do not want you to go to hell. That means I must tell you the whole truth.

I'm sorry, I cannot support your ministry as long as you are embracing a lifestyle that is in opposition to God (nor would I support any other ministry indulging in sinful activity whether they were drunkards, adulterers, thieves, liars, etc.). As a minister and as your friend, I want the absolute best for you. I want to rejoice with you in heaven for all eternity.

The Bible is very clear about homosexuality. Here are some examples from Scripture.

> *That is why God abandoned them to their shameful desires. Even the women turned against the natural way to have sex and instead indulged in sex with each other. And the men, instead of having normal sexual relations with women, burned with lust for each other. Men did shameful things with other men, and as a result of this sin, they suffered within themselves the penalty they deserved.*
> (Romans 1:26-27 NLT)

> *Don't you realize that those who do wrong will not inherit the Kingdom of God? Don't fool yourselves. Those who indulge in sexual sin, or who worship idols, or commit adultery, or are male prostitutes, or practice homosexuality, or are thieves, or greedy people, or drunkards, or are abusive, or cheat people—none of these will inherit the Kingdom of God.*
> (1 Corinthians 6:9-10 NLT)

> *And don't forget Sodom and Gomorrah and their neighboring towns, which were filled with immorality and every kind of sexual perversion. Those cities were destroyed by fire and serve as a warning of the eternal fire of God's judgment.*
> (Jude 1:7 NLT)

But God shows his anger from heaven against all sinful,
wicked people who suppress the truth by their wickedness.
They know the truth about God because he has made it
obvious to them.   (Romans 1:18-19 NLT)

Angel, I share this with you because I care about you. I love
you, and I continue to keep you in my prayers. If you have
any questions, please call me.

I held my breath. I wasn't sure if she would blow up on me and
curse me, or if she would just never respond at all. I checked my
messages frequently until I got this reply:

Miss Donna,

I truly love you and appreciate you. I know it's not right, but
I don't know who else to be. I've been this way since I was
11 years old. I have no other identity.

I became infuriated after reading her message. But I wasn't angry
with Angel. I was angry because of the deception of our enemy—
Satan. So many people are searching for their identities within
the parameters of this imperfect world! That opens the door to
Satan's deception, and yielding to it leads to serious consequences.

It should be clear to Bible-believing Christians that such
powerful deception can end only when deceived hearts are
willing to recognize falsehood, let go of the deceptions they hold,
and yield to God's will for their lives. And that process can begin
only when people understand and accept that their identities
are meant to come from the *Perfect One*—the one and only God
Almighty—who breathed life into our lungs.

Our enemy is masquerading—pretending to have the answers
to all of our problems. And he provides deceptive, false answers
to people's questions.

I wondered if Angel had questions about God's will and her sexuality rolling around in her head as she sat in the church services I led in the jail. If so, I felt accountable for her lack of knowledge. I felt like in order to maintain a comfortable atmosphere, and to keep from sounding like a prude, I had sidestepped a very important issue.

And I felt terrible.

Then Angel replied to me again.

So I can't do anything with this ministry if I'm gay?

Through Angel asking her simple question, I could sense a God-given desire still burning within her to minister to others. But how could I make her understand how serious it is to promote sin in Christ's name? How could I help her?

I breathed a short prayer and then responded to her.

Angel, it is a very dangerous thing to preach Christianity while leading a life in opposition to God. That is why I constantly check myself. We are accountable to God for others who are led astray by our personal actions.

I'm not saying you can't help people, but I would not call it a "Christian" program if you continue to live a homosexual lifestyle. Angel, God wants to use you for His glory. There's no doubt in my mind about that. But He wants you to surrender to His will and leave your past behind.

The enemy of your soul wants you to be confused about your identity. We are all so busy looking for our identities in this fallen world that we have stopped recognizing that our TRUE IDENTITY is in Christ. You were not created to be gay. That is a lie from the enemy to lead your soul into an eternity of destruction.

You were created to shine like a diamond for God's glory. If we want to be His servants and share His Word with power and anointing, we must surrender every part of our lives to Him, including mistaken identities.

Angel, I can't begin to imagine how hard this is for you, because this is not a sin I struggle with personally. But there are plenty of other sins I have struggled with, and I had to make a choice to surrender to God's plan for my life. You will have to make that choice too.

I believe in you, and you better believe I will fight to see you through this, but the decision is yours alone. I can't make it for you. I have seen the real Angel, and she is strong and beautiful, with a testimony that could rescue thousands going through the same struggle. But *you* have to believe in who God called *you* to be.

Want to start over? It's not too late.

Angel responded with a simple, "Okay."

I haven't heard from Angel since then, but I have continued to pray for her.

I also promised to send to her a copy of my friend Keri Cardinale's new book, *Swing Wide.*[9] In that book Keri shares her personal testimony of finding her identity in Christ after living a lesbian lifestyle for many years. I have read it, and I highly recommend her book to anyone who has a friend or family member suffering from identity confusion or those living a homosexual lifestyle.

---

9   *Swing Wide: A Story About Love, Sexual Identity, and How God Redefined it All*, by Keri Cardinale, published by Bridge-Logos, 2019.

After my conversation with Angel, I was extremely convicted over my silence on the topic. I determined right then to go into the jail and share a sermon on sin—all sin—including homosexuality.

And I did.

It was uncomfortable in the beginning, and one lady actually got up and left the service. But before the service ended, many of the ladies thanked me for speaking the truth and teaching them how to minister to their friends who were in homosexual relationships. We have to speak the truth in love, but speak the truth we must!

As I explained to Angel, we must not only accept Christ as our savior but also surrender to His will and let Him begin to transform us into whom He has truly called us to be. In Christ alone, we find our identity.

We all have different temptations to overcome, and Satan is very creative in taking advantage of those temptations and leading people astray. But now it's time to take off the mask, reject the enemy's masquerade, and leave deception behind. And as we do, we also must be willing to lead as many others as possible out of deception when we go.

And so, dear brothers and sisters, I plead with you to give your bodies to God because of all he has done for you. Let them be a living and holy sacrifice—the kind he will find acceptable. This is truly the way to worship him. Don't copy the behavior and customs of this world, but let God transform you into a new person by changing the way you think. Then you will learn to know God's will for you, which is good and pleasing and perfect.

(Romans 12:1-2)

DISCUSSION QUESTIONS

1. Have you ever personally experienced any kind of identity crisis? If so, how were your thoughts affected?

2. Who are we according to 1 John 3:1-2? And as faithful followers, who will we be like?

3. Why do you think the enemy desires to deceive people about their identities?

4. According to Mark 9:42, how does Jesus feel about people who lead others astray?

_____

_____

_____

_____

_____

_____

5. According to Romans 12:1-2, how do we allow God to transform us into a new person?

_____

_____

_____

_____

_____

_____

CHAPTER 3

WELCOMING DECEPTION

THERE IS A lot of deception in this world, and it can wear many different masks and come in many different forms. Generally, by its very definition, deception is unwanted and unpleasant. But some people actually not only willingly embrace and accept it but also welcome it. If you don't believe someone can freely embrace the idea of being deceived, just keep reading.

I know of no one who will admit to willingly allowing himself or herself to be deceived. But when it comes to beliefs, emotions, desires, and matters of the heart, it happens more often than people want to admit.

I was once engaged to be married to a certain man. One day during our engagement, one of my friends shared some devastating news with me about him. She was talking to her friend, Brianna (not her real name), who revealed to her that my fiancé had asked her to go on a date with him.

Brianna had no idea he was engaged to be married to me. She also had no idea she had just shared that information with my best friend. Brianna told my friend she was considering going out with him. When my friend told me the news I was shocked, hurt, heartbroken, and enraged!

I confronted my fiancé with the revelation. Unfortunately, though, I was *blinded by love* and unwilling to give up all I had invested in a two-year relationship, and I allowed my fiancé to convince me it wasn't true.

I was being deceived, but because I loved the relationship I had with him and refused to lose what I thought was mine, I believed his lie. And that set me up for even greater pain in my marriage to him. For after less than one year of marriage, I discovered he was seeing a woman he worked with, and that led to our very painful divorce.

There's an old adage that says, "Fool me once, shame on you. Fool me twice, shame on me!" Well . . .

I can't tell you how many times after my divorce I reflected on the first instance of his infidelity. If I had been wiser in dealing with deception, I could have avoided experiencing the second instance and a future divorce.

Sometimes I believe we embrace deception because it is easier than feeling and accepting pain. But for certain, we can allow ourselves to be deceived because we want to hold on to things that we should let go.

Look around today, and you will see a lot of this kind of denial and reluctance to face and deal with truth—not just specific to relationships, but in all sorts of areas. We always need to face the truth—not avoid it—and allow God to lead us in dealing with it.

Things would have gone differently if I had been willing to surrender my personal desires to the truth God was trying to show me.

As recorded in the gospels, Jesus repeatedly warned His followers to avoid deception. In fact, when the disciples questioned Him about the timing of His return, the first thing Jesus said in His answer to them was, *"Don't let anyone mislead you"* (Matthew 24:4).

Deception is promoted by the enemy of our souls and spread by others who allow themselves to live in deception. And we must be vigilant to keep ourselves from falling in among them and being misled.

But to keep from being misled we must rise above our emotional feelings and desires and take the first step of recognizing deception and realizing where it leads. The following warning Paul shared with Timothy gives us a clear description of the results of not doing that, and those results are rampant in our day.

> *You should know this, Timothy, that in the last days there will be very difficult times. For people will love only themselves and their money. They will be boastful and proud, scoffing at God, disobedient to their parents, and ungrateful. They will consider nothing sacred. They will be unloving and unforgiving; they will slander others and have no self-control. They will be cruel and hate what is good. They will betray their friends, be reckless, be puffed up with pride, and love pleasure rather than God. They will act religious, but they will reject the power that could make them godly. Stay away from people like that!*
>
> (2 Timothy 3:1-5)

We live in a society filled with people who are consumed with their own importance and their possessions. And their selfishness is the driving force behind their disrespect for others. What is important to them is what they have and what they want. Getting what they demand to satisfy their physical desires, emotional needs, and their passions is all that matters to them.

It should not surprise us that such self-centered and prideful people who have lost all sense of decency and respect are willing to accept—even welcome—deception over truth to get their way. And it also should not surprise us that they will choose to follow deceptive teachings of others who themselves have turned to deception to meet their own selfish needs.

We continue reading in Paul's letter to Timothy to see what Paul thought of those teachers.

> *These teachers oppose the truth just as Jannes and Jambres opposed Moses. They have depraved minds and a counterfeit faith.*
>
> (2 Timothy 3:8)

Jesus warned His disciples to not allow themselves to be deceived. And Paul warned Timothy to stay away from people who welcome, live in, and teach deception.

I have studied and repeatedly pondered their warnings. And I have come to believe that false prophets and false teachers would have a lot less authority and influence if we—the Body of Christ—all truly lived the truth, totally surrendered our desires to God, and consciously refused to be deceived.

It is within our power to refuse deception. If Jesus and Paul didn't believe people could refuse to be deceived, they would not have provided their warnings.

But I'm reminded of how easily people accept deception when they are convinced they will gain something from it. We can wish to have or hold on to things so much that our desires cause us to not only accept a lie but also welcome it.

Consuming, uncontrolled desires—that is the definition of lust. Our desires entice us, and if we don't control our desires, they will cause big problems. Instead of controlling our desires, we can be deceived into allowing our desires to control us. And we will pay the consequences for the results.

James tells us what happens when we refuse to deny desires and allow them to lead to sinful behavior.

> *Temptation comes from our own desires, which entice us and drag us away. These desires give birth to sinful actions. And when sin is allowed to grow, it gives birth to death.* (James 1:14-15)

People are dragged away into error by their own uncontrolled desires. And all too often when that happens, they find themselves listening to people living their own lives in deception, false teachers, and deceiving spirits, who will agree with their choices, justify their lusts, and condone their sins. And to the flesh, such validation is truly welcome.

We know the Holy Spirit convicts us of sin and draws us to repentance, and He also continually attempts to keep us out of trouble. But In order to acknowledge the Holy Spirit's wisdom and accept His help, we must first consciously admit our tendency to seek approval for our desires.

We need to pay close attention to the warning Paul gave to Timothy.

> *For a time is coming when people will no longer listen to sound and wholesome teaching. They will follow their own desires and will look for teachers who will tell them whatever their itching ears want to hear. They will reject the truth and chase after myths.* (2 Timothy 4:3-4)

False teachers proliferate whenever there are people willing to follow them. Don't be surprised when false teachers and their deceptive teachings prosper as people who *follow their own desires* seek them out to satisfy what they want to hear and support what they want to do.

It didn't take long in the early days of the Church for false teachers—who claimed to speak for Christ—to form ministries promoting error, or for people to follow them. And people who use their *ministries* to teach lies while claiming to preach God's truth continue doing it today.

Once such ministries are developed and supported, they begin to grow. And they will continue to grow as more and more people welcome the errors they teach to satisfy their personal desires.

That's bad, but even worse is knowing that many innocent people really seeking truth (but who are not well-founded in the Word) will often go wherever they see ministries appearing to flourish. And while they may not initially have the same itchy ears as others, over time they too can fall prey to error.

We must not become guilty of helping false teachers increase their influence.

The Bible contains many warnings about false teachers and false prophets. Read the Bible and stay close to what it says. We must not yield our minds and emotions to something that sounds good but is destructive to our lives and relationship with God.

But there were also false prophets in Israel, just as there will be false teachers among you. They will cleverly teach destructive heresies and even deny the Master who bought them. In this way, they will bring sudden destruction on themselves. Many will follow their evil teaching and shameful immorality. And because of these teachers, the way of truth will be slandered. In their greed they will make up clever lies to get hold of your money. But God condemned them long ago, and their destruction will not be delayed. (2 Peter 2:1-3)

Is it a new thing for false teachers to *make up clever lies to get hold of your money?* Absolutely not. False prophets and teachers have always thrived on influence and greed, and they still want people's money today more than they want to represent God's truth. Peter went on to describe what the false teachers are like.

These people are as useless as dried-up springs or as mist blown away by the wind. They are doomed to blackest darkness. They brag about themselves with empty, foolish boasting. With an appeal to twisted sexual desires, they lure back into sin those who have barely escaped from a lifestyle of deception. They promise freedom, but they themselves are slaves of sin and corruption. For you are a slave to whatever controls you. And when people escape from the wickedness of the world by knowing our Lord and Savior Jesus Christ and then get tangled up and enslaved by sin again, they are worse off than before. (2 Peter 2:17-20)

I can't help but notice in Peter's words his mention of the *appeal to twisted sexual desires.*

If we take a look into the past, those of us who are older—or more seasoned—can remember a time when sex outside of marriage was not accepted as normal by society. I can remember a time when people didn't boast about engaging in sexual activity outside of marriage. It was considered shameful—as sin should be.

The way it has been portrayed for years, though, sex outside of marriage is something that everyone has been doing. And a large percentage of those living today no longer consider it shameful. It is now embraced as normal. But contending it is normal is false teaching. False teachers say things are OK. These things are expected. But that's not God's expectation.

Many people have accepted the lie that sexual activity outside of marriage is not sinful. They don't *want* to believe it is sinful.

They want to continue indulging their immoral, sexual desires without guilt. So they look for and welcome the teachings of those who will agree with them. But God's Word has not changed. Our personal views of fornication—sexual activity outside of marriage—will not cause it to become acceptable to Christ.

Once a society is deceived into accepting and embracing one sin, it opens the door for accepting more. After sexual activity outside of marriage became acceptable to the masses, it wasn't long before homosexuality literally started *coming out of the closet*. Sin that was once considered shameful and hidden behind closed doors began to weave its web of deception, so that it too could be embraced in society.

People began to welcome yet another lie so they could live out their desires with no shame. Promoters of same-sex relationships gained positions of influence. The politics of power triumphed over reason, and society at large began to be pressured into embracing more and more deception. Now false teachers preach the lie that homosexuality is normal, acceptable, and even to be celebrated in same-sex marriage.

Deception breeds deception. And people come to love and welcome lies in order to hold on to their sin and experience no shame. However, accepting lies and welcoming deception does not empty sins of their consequences.

Here is another warning from Paul about false teachers and deception in the last days:

> *Now the Holy Spirit tells us clearly that in the last times some will turn away from the true faith; they will follow deceptive spirits and teachings that come from demons. These people are hypocrites and liars, and their consciences are dead.* (1 Timothy 4:1-2)

There is no doubt that the enemy and his demons promote deception. However, Satan and his evil minions cannot force deception on anyone who is not willing to be deceived. People who know, believe, and hold to the truth—those who refuse to welcome their demonic lies—will not be deceived.

In light of all of the warnings about deception in the last days, we *must* know and study the Word of God. We must stand on God's truth. We must deny ourselves and any desires that war against truth. We must be willing to surrender our lives completely to Christ.

Paul's words to the Ephesians serve as a good reminder to us today. We should hold tightly to the truth that comes from Jesus alone.

> *With the Lord's authority I say this: Live no longer as the Gentiles do, for they are hopelessly confused. Their minds are full of darkness; they wander far from the life God gives because they have closed their minds and hardened their hearts against him. They have no sense of shame. They live for lustful pleasure and eagerly practice every kind of impurity.*
>
> *But that isn't what you learned about Christ. Since you have heard about Jesus and have learned the truth that comes from him, throw off your old sinful nature and your former way of life, which is corrupted by lust and deception. Instead, let the Spirit renew your thoughts and attitudes. Put on your new nature, created to be like God—truly righteous and holy.*   (Ephesians 4:17-24)

We must not only personally adhere to truth and reject lies and deception, we must make a serious effort to examine the words and lives of people who present themselves as speaking truth to us. Not everyone who says he or she speaks for God actually does. And today, more and more people who say they promote Christianity and God's will on things actually promote lies.

Today, many false prophets and teachers claim God's authority when they reinforce the legitimacy of lifestyles that are contrary to Scripture by telling people what they want to hear. Jesus spoke about how to recognize them.

> *Beware of false prophets who come disguised as harmless sheep but are really vicious wolves. You can identify them by their fruit, that is, by the way they act. Can you pick grapes from thorn bushes, or figs from thistles?* (Matthew 7:15-16)

We must be fruit inspectors, especially regarding the opinions and teachings we accept—and regarding those people to whom we listen. We should be like the Bereans, who eagerly listened to Paul's teaching but also searched the Scriptures daily to be sure he and Silas were teaching them the truth. We must be on guard—quick to recognize false doctrine masquerading as truth.

John also addressed this when he wrote about recognizing the deception of false prophets.

> *Dear friends, do not believe everyone who claims to speak by the Spirit. You must test them to see if the spirit they have comes from God. For there are many false prophets in the world.*
>
> *. . .*
>
> *But you belong to God, my dear children. You have already won a victory over those people, because the Spirit who lives in you is greater than the spirit who lives in the world. Those people belong to this world, so they speak from the world's viewpoint, and the world listens to them. But we belong to God, and those who know God listen to us. If they do not belong to God, they do not listen to us. That is how we know if someone has the Spirit of truth or the spirit of deception.* (1 John 4:1-6)

We must know the Word and hold fast to what the Holy Spirit reveals to us through it. And we absolutely must desire the revelation of truth and be determined to follow it even if it means our flesh's expectations of the present and dreams of the future are disappointed.

We must choose truth over satisfying our wants and wishes.

We must desire and live in truth and not allow ourselves to be willingly blinded by refusing to acknowledge and deal with the pain that the truth can bring to our flesh as a result of facing either our mistakes or those of others. We must not allow our flesh to influence us to be deceived by either the enemy of our souls or our own fleshly desires.

As we go about attempting to satisfy our desires, we must allow God to instruct us and empower us to fight against and become victors over anything that tempts us to go beyond God's will. We must put our desires under the control of the Holy Spirit and not deceive ourselves into trusting in the so-called wisdom of the flesh.

As we surrender our lives completely to the will of God and seek to please Him, we can finally reject any thought that deception is ever desirable. Then, as we live close to the truth, we are prepared to avoid deception's traps.

And the best words of advice on how to become so close to the truth that we do not allow the flesh to embrace or welcome deception in any way are contained in Paul's instructions to Timothy (and these words are so important to act on as we also attempt to teach others to avoid deception).

Study to [show yourself] approved unto God, a workman that [doesn't need] to be ashamed, rightly dividing the word of truth.
(2 Timothy 2:15 KJV)[10]

10 With updated language by this author as bracketed.

DISCUSSION QUESTIONS

1. Can you think of a time when you would have preferred to believe a lie (anything less than the full truth) rather than face the facts? How would you have benefited from believing that lie?

2. Looking back to 2 Timothy 3:1-5, which of Paul's descriptions of things to come can you identify in our current society? Which one stands out most to you?

3. How did Jesus describe Satan as recorded in John 8:44?

4. According to 1 John 4:4-6, how can we know if someone has the Spirit of truth or a spirit of deception?

_____

_____

_____

_____

_____

_____

5. As recorded in Matthew 24:24, who did Jesus say false prophets will be able to lead astray if possible?

_____

_____

_____

_____

_____

_____

6. According to Romans 16:18, who else also may be deceived, and why?

_____

_____

_____

_____

_____

CHAPTER 4

EVEN THE CHOSEN

IN MY OPINION, one of the most disturbing Scriptures in the Bible comes from Matthew chapter twenty-four. Jesus was talking to His disciples in verse twenty-four of that chapter and answering a question they had about what to expect in the future. This is what He said:

> *For false messiahs and false prophets will rise up and perform great signs and wonders so as to deceive, if possible, even God's chosen ones.* (Matthew 24:24)

The New International Version of the Bible uses the words "the elect" in place of *God's chosen ones.* The King James Version uses the phrase, "the very elect." Merriam Webster defines elect as "carefully selected: CHOSEN," or "one chosen or set apart (as by divine favor)."[11]

---

11 https://www.merriam-webster.com/dictionary/elect

This verse provides a warning to God's *chosen ones*. For sure, Jesus was talking to His disciples, but it becomes clear as we read all of what Jesus had to say that His words are meant to be received by all of His followers, not just His disciples that day. Jesus' words inform us—all of us—that we must be wary of being deceived.

So within Jesus' words in answering His disciples' questions about end-time events, we see a warning for all believers to be aware of false messiahs and false prophets—even if they perform great signs and wonders. But the warning is given more weight when we think about those who have been carefully selected or set apart—such as the disciples who walked with Him that day—falling to deception.

For sure, regardless of our places in the Kingdom, we must all take note of Jesus' warning.

Reflecting on the Lord's words in verse twenty-four causes me to think of another disturbing passage that is closely related to it. It is also found in Matthew.

> *On judgment day many will say to me, "Lord! Lord! We prophesied in your name and cast out demons in your name and performed many miracles in your name." But I will reply, "I never knew you. Get away from me, you who break God's laws."*
>
> (Matthew 7:22-23)

Clearly, those who say they teach or speak for God—even those whose words have been seemingly confirmed by performing miracles—have a critical responsibility to avoid deception, live up to God's expectations, and not fall into being a tool of the enemy that leads others into error.

Although all believers—who are all chosen—should take to heart the message of this chapter, there is a particular point of interest within it for those in positions of leadership. No one, regardless of position, should allow himself or herself to be led into deception.

Something that disturbs me most about the passage in Matthew chapter twenty-four is what I see as a logical extension of reasoning when taking into account Jesus' words. For if there are false messiahs and false prophets who deceive others through performing signs and wonders, it is clear that they were, themselves, first deceived.

And the depth of their deception is illustrated in Jesus' statement in chapter seven. Even if we are doing the very things God has chosen or set us apart to do, we should heed Jesus' warning about how people can be deceived.

Far too many people today—including far too many spiritual leaders—are seemingly unaware they themselves are living in deception. As I pondered why God can allow them to do what they do and use His name in the first place if they are not completely devoted to God's truth, I believe He showed me some things in His Word.

Flipping through my Bible I was compelled to stop at chapter thirteen of the first book of Kings. I will summarize it as I point out what I believe God was showing me. If you are not familiar with this chapter, I encourage you to read it for yourself.

We read in the book of Kings that King Jeroboam was an evil king who had built idols and set up shrines on high places for worshiping idols.

And contrary to God's instructions to the Israelites, Jeroboam also appointed people to be priests who were not descendants of Levi (contrary to God's instructions for the priesthood). He then instituted a festival on the fifteenth day of the eighth month to offer sacrifices to his idols on the altar he built at Bethel.[12]

So God sent a prophet—a man of God from Judah (we never find out his name)—to deliver a word from the Lord. He went to Bethel during Jeroboam's pagan festival and delivered a word from God. He spoke that day just as Jeroboam was approaching the altar to burn incense.

> *Then at the LORD's command, he shouted, "O altar, altar! This is what the LORD says: A child named Josiah will be born into the dynasty of David. On you he will sacrifice the priests from the pagan shrines who come here to burn incense, and human bones will be burned on you."* (1 Kings 13:2)

The man of God spoke to that altar of sacrifice and prophesied of the future actions of Josiah—a king who would not be born for another three hundred years—who would destroy the priests of the high places and burn their bones on the altar there at Bethel.

Then the man of God gave them a sign that he spoke with the authority of God.

> *That same day the man of God gave a sign to prove his message. He said, "The LORD has promised to give this sign: This altar will split apart, and its ashes will be poured out on the ground."* (1 Kings 13:3)

At this, King Jeroboam told his guards to seize the man. But when he pointed at the man of God, the king's hand was paralyzed so that he could not move it. Then, immediately, *"a wide crack appeared in the altar, and the altar split apart and the ashes poured out, just as the man of God had predicted in his message from the LORD"* (v.5).

---

12 1 Kings 12:31-33.

King Jeroboam began to plead with the man of God to ask his God to heal his hand. So the man of God prayed, and miraculously, the king's hand was healed. The king then invited the man of God to come to his palace. He promised to give the man something to eat and drink there and give him a gift.

Pay attention to the resolve of the man of God in what followed.

> But the man of God said to the king, "Even if you gave me half of everything you own, I would not go with you. I would not eat or drink anything in this place. For the LORD gave me this command: 'You must not eat or drink anything while you are there, and do not return to Judah by the same way you came.'"
>
> (1 Kings 13:8-9)

The man of God told the king that he wouldn't go with him even if he gave him half of everything he owned! That certainly took some resolve don't you think?

I can't help but think that his resolve to do God's will was increased after he experienced God *using him* to accomplish the mighty signs that had just taken place. We are often filled with refreshed resolve when we feel God has used us to do something special. And as a minister, I have learned it can happen when we leave a church service where the Holy Spirit has moved in a powerful way through our ministries.

What amazes me, though, is how quickly that man of God's resolve vanished a short time later when he allowed himself to be deceived.

As we continue reading, we read about an old prophet who lived there in Bethel. He heard about what the man of God did, and he immediately wanted to meet the man. So he told his sons to saddle up his donkey, and he left on the donkey to find him.

When he arrived where the man of God was, he found him sitting beneath a tree.

The old prophet invited the man of God to come home with him to eat some food. Once again the man of God repeated what God had told him—to not eat or drink in that place. But the old prophet had a response for the man, and it was a mixture of truth and fiction.

> But the old prophet answered, "I am a prophet, too, just as you are. And an angel gave me this command from the LORD: 'Bring him home with you so he can have something to eat and drink.'" But the old man was lying to him. (1 Kings 13:18)

The old prophet first told the man of God that he himself was a prophet, which was true. But then he told a lie. He had not heard from God, and God had not sent an angel to him with a message for the man. The old prophet himself was caught up in deceiving someone—even a man of God.

And unfortunately, the man of God allowed himself to be convinced to go with him. He accepted the old prophet's lie and shared a meal with him. And then, as they were eating, the old prophet actually received a true word from God and told the man that he had defied the word of the Lord.

> He cried out to the man of God from Judah, "This is what the LORD says: You have defied the word of the LORD and have disobeyed the command the LORD your God gave you. You came back to this place and ate and drank where he told you not to eat or drink. Because of this, your body will not be buried in the grave of your ancestors." (I Kings 13:21-22)

After the man of God left the old prophet's home, as the man was traveling down the road, he was killed by a lion and left on the road dead. And when the old prophet was told about what happened, he went to get the man's body, and he buried him in his own grave as he cried out in grief, *"Oh, my brother!"* [13]

Many people want to place all of the blame squarely on the old prophet for deceiving the man of God. But it appears that after he knowingly told a big lie to deceive the man of God, he just went on with his life with no consequence while the man of God paid for his disobedience with his early demise. It doesn't seem fair.

But now or later, we will all answer for our actions—even that old prophet. And here, I simply think it's important to note that even prophets and preachers can get it wrong.

Dealing with the story gets even more challenging when we consider that, despite his recent failure, God still used the lying prophet to speak judgment over the man of God at his house while they were eating. God's grace is clearly not like the grace we are apt to extend to people who fail us.

But let's look a little deeper into the story. As we do, we should be able to see that each of the men was responsible for his own actions.

While the prophet was guilty of lying, that did not excuse the man of God for his actions.

I wish I knew what was going through the man of God's mind as he sat under that tree before the old prophet approached him. Was he reveling in the fact that God had used him in a powerful way? There's nothing wrong with rejoicing in that, of course. It's thrilling when God uses us for His glory. [14] But was his success affecting his views in a negative way?

---

13 1 Kings 13:27-30.

14 Of course there is a limit to how we should allow our emotions to affect our actions and pride. "When the seventy-two disciples returned, they joyfully reported to him, 'Lord, even the demons obey us when we use your name!' 'Yes,' he told them . . .. 'But don't rejoice because evil spirits obey you; rejoice because your names are registered in heaven'" (Luke 10:17-20).

Was something going on in his mind that could eventually be used to convince him to yield to deception? We have no idea what he was thinking. But we know that God had given him orders to avoid eating or drinking anything in that place. And the man repeated those orders out loud to others when he was offered a meal—twice.

The man knew what God had said to him. So why would he come to believe a complete stranger who contradicted what he was told—a stranger who claimed to hear a contradictory message from God for him?

The man of God was clearly capable of hearing from God. God told him to prophesy over that altar, and the altar was split in half, with the ashes pouring out just as God had said. He had seen God confirm His Word just a short time earlier. He knew God was faithful to do what He said He would do.

So why did he take the word of the old prophet over what God had personally told him? Why couldn't the man discern whether or not the prophet was telling him the truth?

He had to have realized that the word of the old prophet completely contradicted the Lord's instructions to him. Did he take a moment to ask God if He had indeed sent the old prophet to him? How quickly it appears he took the old man's word for truth and gave it precedence over what God had told him!

The man of God had walked a long way. He was probably hungry, and I'm sure he was thirsty too. But he resisted the king's offer when the king asked him to come and eat. He resisted the king because he had received a direct order from God, and he was determined to obey it.

So why was the king unable to convince him to eat and drink, but the prophet speaking a lie was able to do it? Why was the man of God not able to muster the same resolve to trust what God had told him when he was confronted by the old prophet's words?

These are good questions, and considering them will help us see some things.

First, we can see that the king was not trying to deceive the man of God. The king couldn't deny what happened after the man delivered God's words. And he couldn't refute how the man prayed to God for the king's healing, and he was healed. The king was simply responding with a normal sense of gratitude and amazement over what had just taken place.

Clearly, there was something similar in both the king's and the old prophet's invitations. Both of the invitation's appealed to the man's desires. But unlike the king's invitation, when the old prophet spoke he claimed to have heard from God on the matter. And in that, a door was opened to a particularly insidious form of deception.

The man of God knew the king did not serve God. Since the man of God was a true believer, it is not difficult to accept that he would be able to resist the request of someone he knew to be living an evil and disobedient life. But when confronted by someone who was supposed to be a spiritual leader—and one who claimed to have heard from God—it was a different story.

We should be more inclined to listen and accept the words, or advice, of believers—people who are connected to God. We should seriously consider their words. But we must understand that even they do not have the authority to override the clear instructions that God himself has given to us.

The man of God knew the Lord was fully capable of speaking directly to him. If God had changed His mind, He could have spoken to the man of God again and told him to go and eat with the prophet. But God didn't do that. God's true word to the man did not change.

Sadly, the man of God made a decision to believe the old prophet's words, and he allowed himself to be deceived. People today continue to be led into deception by others who claim to have a word from God but do not. We must hold on to what God has already revealed to us and not allow others—regardless of their spiritual claims—to lead us astray by contradicting God's directions.

I'm reminded of an instance when I was in a church service praying for people as the Holy Spirit led me. A lady walked up to me, put her finger in my face, and said, "God told me to tell you to go pray for that man in the back pew."

At first I started to go to him, but the Holy Spirit checked me. I stopped in my tracks, turned and looked at the lady, and said, "God didn't tell *me* to go and pray for that man. Perhaps he wants you to instead."

When anyone claims to have a word from God for you, you must be sure, first and foremost, that the word lines up with the Word of God—the Holy Bible. If it contradicts Scripture in any way, you know there is an attempt to deceive you. But even if it passes the Scripture test, ask yourself if God is truly speaking that word from another person to your own heart.

Does it resonate with your spirit? Does the Holy Spirit confirm to you it is from God?

God confirms His words to us by His Spirit within us. After first instinctively starting to go pray for someone, I suddenly realized that regardless of what claim the lady made about hearing from God, in no way did I feel that God wanted me to go and pray for the man.

I'm not saying God doesn't use other people to speak to us. He most certainly does. But at that point, I was carefully listening for the voice of God. He had a direct line of communication with *me*.

And when that lady came to me with her *word*, it did not resonate at all as God's word to me.

We must make Scripture and God's personal orders to us our top priorities. Looking back at the man of God and his situation recorded in First Kings, I continued to ponder exactly why he would dismiss the word of God he received and accept the word of a stranger. It didn't take me long to come to a conclusion.

Using deceptive words is one of the enemy's oldest strategies. The enemy has been using them since shortly after the creation of man. When Satan approached Eve in the Garden of Eden he didn't just pluck a piece of fruit from the tree and try to get her to eat it. He didn't force the fruit into her hand or her mouth. He merely put a question in her mind.

He just asked her a simple question. "Did God *really* say . . . ?" (Genesis 3:1).[15]

The enemy and his evil influences start by trying to get us to question what God said. Satan opposes what God said, and he knows that when we begin to doubt what God really said, we set ourselves up to be deceived.

We must know God. We must know His character as revealed in the Bible. We must recognize His voice. And we must not only know but also trust His word delivered to us so no one can persuade us to believe something God didn't really say.

Paul warned the people at Galatia about believing anything that opposes the truth of what God had already revealed to them.

I am astonished that you are so quickly deserting the one who called you to live in the grace of Christ and are turning to a different gospel—which is really no gospel at all. Evidently some people are throwing you into confusion and are trying to pervert

---

15 When addressing Satan's deceptive nature it is difficult to not make full use of such a powerful illustration as his words to Eve in the garden. I use his words and the garden story again in the ninth chapter to address *division*.

the gospel of Christ. But even if we or an angel from heaven should preach a gospel other than the one we preached to you, let them be under God's curse! As we have already said, so now I say again: If anybody is preaching to you a gospel other than what you accepted, let them be under God's curse!

(Galatians 1:6-9 NIV)

Preacher or layman, we must not think for a moment that we are above being deceived. Jesus warned that even the *chosen* could be deceived, and we must believe it.

We have been chosen and set apart as a people—a royal priesthood who should know and speak truth to a world that is terribly deceived. We cannot be tripped up by questioning for one second the importance and authority of what God has said. His Word—the Bible—is both the first and final authority. We must stand firm behind its words against deception in any form, no matter where or who it comes from.

We must also realize that even though God chooses to use us for His purposes—even in amazing ways—we can still be deceived and pay an awful price for disobeying if we become disobedient to what God says.

God is Sovereign. He decides whom He uses. And it will help us stay humble to remember that God will use even evil kings and others with influence to bring about the things He wants to accomplish. But His use of them does not automatically indicate His approval of the way they live, and we must understand that.

We must make sure we are following God with all our hearts and obeying all His commands. In this way we will know we continue to be in the will of God.[16]

It is our responsibility to hear what the Holy Spirit is telling us and reject what He is not. We must hear from God, be obedient

---

16 "Our actions will show that we belong to the truth, so we will be confident when we stand before God" (1 John 3:19).

to what He has told us, and not allow ourselves to be persuaded to cast aside His instructions to us.

Our confidence to know and follow God—and our possession of the kind of intimate relationship with Him that makes that possible—begins (and ultimately ends) with knowing and obeying the words of the Bible.

But regardless of whether His word to us comes from Scripture or the personal guidance He confirms to us by the Holy Spirit, the word He gives to us is a lamp to guide our feet and a light for our paths.[17] And allowing His words to shine continually and unhindered by deceptive words in our lives will prevent us from going astray.

Regardless of whether we are leaders or those being led, we are believers. And believers must recognize and reject lies masquerading as God's instructions. We are *God's chosen ones*, but even the chosen must sometimes be reminded to never stop learning to recognize God's voice and always study and hold obediently to God's truths. Doing these things will ensure that we do not succumb to deception!

DISCUSSION QUESTIONS

1. In Matthew 24:24, Jesus warned His own disciples—those who walked with Him, those who saw His miracles, and heard His teaching—about being deceived by false prophets. Why do you think we should be even more perceptive to deception in this day and age?

---

17 Psalm 119:105.

2. How do you feel when you read Jesus' words in Matthew 7:22-23?

3. What can we learn about God's sovereignty when we read about the old prophet still being used by God *after* he lied to the man of God?

4. Why do you think Satan tries to get us to question what God says in His Word?

5. Can you think of a time when you were tempted to question what God really said in His Word? If so, was the question in regard to what His Word reveals to us about a particular sin?

_____

_____

_____

_____

_____

_____

6. Can you identify three ways many members of society have been deceived by the enemy today? What are they?

_____

_____

_____

_____

_____

_____

CHAPTER 5

A DEADLY DECEPTION

ACCORDING TO A November 27, 2019, article written by Michael New and printed in National Review, a 2012 study published in the *Southern Medical Journal* analyzed more than 170,000 women in California who either had an abortion or gave birth to a child. The study found that the women in the study group who had an abortion were one hundred fifty-four percent (154%) more likely to commit suicide than women who gave birth.

Michael New's article addressed the findings in a recent study published in the British medical journal, *The Lancet*. The authors of that study contended the more recent British study disproved the link between abortion and suicide among pregnant women. In his article, Mr. New pointed out serious flaws in the newer British study and listed studies conducted in both Italy and Finland, the results of which were consistent with the 2012 California study.[18]

---

18 https://www.nationalreview.com/corner/new-lancet-study-fails-to-disprove-abortion-suicide-link/

Since the 1973 Supreme Court decision that legalized abortion in the United States, vast numbers of women have had abortions. And that means their decisions led to the death of a corresponding vast number of babies. According to statistics published on Wikipedia, over 45.7 million abortions were performed in the United States from 1970 through 2015.[19] Written out, that number of abortions is **45,700,000**. And many more have been carried out since then.

The numbers are staggering in the United States, alone, but when we consider abortion numbers worldwide it should make our head spin and shake us to the core.

The value of human life should be uncontested. No one should be deceived by any argument that devalues any human life regardless of whether the life is inside or outside the womb. Think about the ramifications and seriousness of procreation and pregnancy contained in King David's words recorded in the book of Psalms.

> *For you created my inmost being; you knit me together in my mother's womb. ... Your eyes saw my unformed body; all the days ordained for me were written in your book before one of them came to be.* (Psalm 139:13-16 NIV)

How tragic that God's careful nurturing of so many innocents and His plans for their lives have been ignored and thwarted by the decisions of their mothers. And consider how deep the deception is that led them to make those decisions!

In a society so consumed with campaigning for the rights of individuals, it is sadly ironic that people overlook or actually choose to ignore the rights of the most innocent. The enemy has used many tools to deceive people into thinking abortion is a

19 https://en.wikipedia.org/wiki/Abortion_statistics_in_the_United_States

legitimate expression of freedom, but that expression has led to much destruction.

So many women have been convinced that, "Because it's my body, it's my right to terminate my pregnancy."

Many women have been lulled into a false sense of justification for having an abortion as agencies such as Planned Parenthood have tried to make people believe that a fetus is just a mass of cells. And as the lies have been propagated and declared as truth, many have experienced dire circumstances by believing them.

The aftermath of abortion is downplayed, and many women suffer in silence—feeling as though they are alone. Many women experience depression and anxiety after having abortions, and some are even driven to attempt suicide because of the guilt they experience. Many women's lives are ruined because of one fateful decision—to take the lives of their own children.

Sherry Hopper, of Sherry Hopper Ministries, has a powerful ministry speaking up for the unborn. She is a dear friend, and as I was talking to her some time back she shared her heart-wrenching story with me.

I asked Sherry for permission to use her testimony in this book, and she is allowing me to share it with you. This is her testimony that she shared with me in her own words:

> I was a troubled teen. Having suffered many years of sexual abuse at the hands of my father and other men, I had a few issues—to say the least. At the age of fifteen, I became pregnant by my boyfriend. The abuse had ended only about a year prior to that.

I was in deep counseling several times a week and fully aware of most of my issues. I knew one thing for sure; I did *not* know what to do. I immediately started seeking counsel for this new issue—pregnancy.

I was scared to make the wrong decision, and I knew I didn't know how to make a good decision at that point in my life. I knew my options were to keep the child, put it up for adoption, or have an abortion.

Over my entire life, even as a young girl, I was devoted to never hurting my child. I was going to be the best mother ever. I was determined that my child would never hurt from my own doings or anyone else's if I could help it. Even if I never did anything worthwhile in my own life, my children would know without a doubt how much I loved them!

I went to each of my counseling team members—counselors, psychologists, and psychiatrists—to get their advice about what to do. They couldn't by law advise me, but they promised to support me in whatever I decided.

I spoke with my mother and told her I didn't know what to do. She told me that if I decided to keep the child, she would help me raise it, but if I decided to abort the pregnancy, she would pay for half the cost of the abortion, and my boyfriend's mother could cover the other half. She told me it was my decision, but she would support me in whatever I decided.

Planned Parenthood had a huge facility in Memphis, Tennessee, where I had gone for a while to obtain birth control. I knew they did abortions there. I also knew many of my friends had chosen to have abortions for unwanted pregnancies, but I was not sure about having one myself. I didn't know the details of abortion.

My biggest concerns were, "When does a baby actually *become* a baby? What are the risks? Does it hurt?" I had many questions that I didn't have the answers to.

I finally went to Planned Parenthood—the only place I knew to seek answers to these vitally important questions. They were the experts in planning for parenting; they were pro-family and pro-woman—or so I thought. They knew me, and I *felt* I knew them. I trusted them. I thought they were a loving organization.

I met with a counselor there and told her my concerns about the baby. I asked her a lot of questions, like, "When does life begin? Can the baby feel anything? When is it more than just a cluster of cells?"

She reached across her desk, took my hand, and said, "Oh honey, the last thing you need is a child. You need to work on yourself. The fetus is just a cluster of cells. It can't feel anything." She was as sweet and caring as could be.

She continued, "We only have until next week, when you'll be twelve weeks pregnant, to do the procedure. So you need to make a decision today. We need to book you before it's too late."

I booked that day for early the next week and left the facility.

As I spoke with the Planned Parenthood counselor, I felt she really cared about me. I honestly still do. She thought she was doing the best thing for me. Years later I considered that her eyes were just blinded to the truth, and in time

God spoke to me to confirm that. It took me many years to forgive her, but I have.

I went through the procedure the following week, only a few days after my initial visit. I asked to see the fetus to make sure it wasn't a baby—to confirm I had made the right decision. The doctor was very hateful in his words to me and refused to allow me to see it. I know now that was a *God thing*. I would have never been able to get that image out of my mind.

A couple of weeks later, the local newspaper carried an advertisement from a pro-life organization regarding what a fetus looks like at twelve weeks. In the image the baby was sucking his thumb, had ten fingers and ten toes, and experienced hiccups. My baby was approximately this age when it was aborted.

My **baby**. It **was** a baby, not a fetus. I hate the word *fetus* now. It's so dehumanizing.

Upon looking at the images in the advertisement, I immediately knew what I had done. I had murdered my child. Even worse than that, I had *paid* someone to murder my child. I again had been lied to, and again I had paid the ultimate price for it.

No, my baby paid the ultimate price for the deception.

I refused to accept that. I wanted to die! I deserved to die! Regardless of the decision, it was mine, and I had made it.

Sinking lower and lower into depression, I decided to attempt suicide. By God's grace, my mother caught me as I attempted to kill myself, and she admitted me into a medical facility for troubled youth. They saved my life by teaching me coping skills and prescribing medication.

I was told I would never be healed because of the damage that was done to my brain from the trauma. They said I'd have to take the medications for the rest of my life or the symptoms would resurface. Following that, I fought suicide and depression for over *thirty years.*

But God!

I was completely delivered from suicide and depression at the age of forty-five after giving everything to God. God dealt with me about forgiving myself for the abortion. He then delivered me from its effects.

I haven't taken another pill, nor have I suffered another moment since then. God is the God of healing—and the *Father* who loves and forgives. He has never deceived me nor left me. Ultimately, He was the one I was seeking—the one with the solution. He has made me whole!

—Sherry Hopper, Sherry Hopper Ministries[20]

Sherry Hopper has a powerful testimony that illustrates both the insidiousness of human reasoning and God's ability to overcome it. Surely it was God who, in His grace, arranged for Sherry's mother to intervene in Sherry's attempt to take her life. And it was a display of God's grace and His enduring love that finally brought to Sherry her total solution.

However, as Sherry wrote, even after being rescued from her attempted suicide she continued to suffer for her decision many

---

20 Sherry now shares her testimony of God's grace with women at conferences and other events. Though the enemy sought to destroy her life through the deception of abortion and its effects, God rescued her. God is now using her life to help other women find hope and healing. To learn more about Sherry's ministry, visit her website at *https://www.sherryhopper.com/*.

years and had to turn to medications to survive the psychological results of yielding to the world's deceptive thinking. The decision to abort a baby is indeed deadly, and it has long effects. But we are blessed to have a Father in heaven who will forgive us and rescue us when we yield to deception.

I am blessed to know a few amazing ladies with testimonies of surviving the deception surrounding abortion. Another one of them is my dear friend, Sheila Harper. She and her husband, Jack, are making a huge impact on this world by sharing the truth about the devastating effects of abortion. Sheila also shared her testimony with me for this chapter, and I now share it with you.

When I was four years old, my mother and I were in a tragic car accident. I was thrown through the windshield and recovered from my injuries, but my mother was killed instantly.

Following that event—during my early childhood years—I endured sexual abuse. And a psychotic stepmother came into the picture. She hated me and made sure I knew it. Then, when I was eleven years old, I was sent to live with my aunt and uncle.

Although my uncle was an alcoholic, those were the happiest, most endearing years of my young life. My uncle wasn't your typical alcoholic but rather a charisma-filled, eccentric charmer who was always the life of the party. Or at least that's how I remember him.

He and my aunt made my life fun again. It was during those years when I accepted Jesus Christ as my Savior. I was only twelve, but I knew exactly what I was doing.

Throughout my teen years I lived for the Lord and made it all the way through high school as a *good girl*. It was only after I started college when I made decisions that I knew weren't good for me.

At the time, I wanted to have some fun. So I packed up God in a neat little box and put Him on a shelf. With me at the reins of my life, it didn't take long for me to steer my life right off a cliff. Within the year, I entered into a relationship I had no business being in, and six months later I was pregnant.

Everything in me said abortion was wrong, but I charged forward with really bad advice—accepted from even the worst of friends—and I went through with it anyway. March 29, 1985, was the day of my most regrettable mistake. I was nineteen years old and making decisions of life and death that I had no business making.

My boyfriend broke up with me shortly after that, and I really don't blame him. He begged me not to have the abortion, but I selfishly did anyway. Don't ever let anyone tell you abortion is just a woman's issue. Men suffer from the aftermath of the choice as well.

For seven years after the abortion, my life became a mess. I started drinking and consuming vast amounts of drugs. I spent all my money going to concerts and getting backstage. I signed up for credit cards and maxed them out. I suffered through a rape, and I went through relationships like water—not committing to anything or anybody.

I became consumed with death—hoping that if I took enough drugs, or drank enough alcohol, I wouldn't wake up. After an attempted suicide and being consumed with wanting to die, I met a man in a bar and cleaned myself up enough to get married.

My husband, Jack, is the real hero in all of this. He loved me even when I was so messed up, and he lived with the drama of my life for years.

We had two sons right away. I have always felt like my first son was a gift from God used to wake me up. That pregnancy got my attention and made me realize my life was worth living—if not for myself, then for this precious creature that had been entrusted to me.

My second son was born on the twenty-ninth of March, the anniversary of the very day I had taken a life. To me, on that very day God gave me another gift straight from Him.

God speaks often, heals much, and redirects life's circumstances through children and pregnancies. Jack and I just celebrated thirty-one years of marriage. After having spent the last three decades with him—enjoying life, making memories, raising two awesomely incredible boys, and basically growing up together—I can truly say I'm completely blessed.

Not long into our marriage, I heard about a class that was being offered for women who had experienced abortion and were having trouble afterward. I couldn't believe it. I was so happy to find an outlet for my emotions and the pain that I could never fully deal with.

Being in a group with others who had suffered like experiences after abortion brought sense to everything and helped me understand those seven years of being isolated and alone. The group did a Bible study, and it gave me back my life. It showed me how I needed to accept Jesus' forgiveness and forgive myself.

Meeting with the group was an incredible time of discovery, and the study brought to me a much-needed transformation.

Meeting God through that study—meeting Him in a way I had never known—inspired me. I immediately felt compelled to start teaching the class to others. I wanted women and men who were suffering after abortion to know and experience the same forgiveness and freedom I was experiencing.

I enjoyed teaching the class for several years. Finally, in the year 2000, God started showing me the need for an abortion recovery ministry. I started that ministry—*SaveOne*—and since that time, my wildest dreams have come true.

I have never had more fun in my entire life than after I finally surrendered all to God. To see God take my most regrettable mistake and turn it around to help others find freedom through truth is an unexplainable joy. Through SaveOne, we now help women, men, and families around the world recover after abortion.

After starting the ministry, God gave me my first book to write, *SaveOne: A Guide to Emotional Healing after Abortion.* It's a guide for women to enable them to work through the aftermath of having an abortion. Shortly after the first book was published, the Lord led me to write *SaveOne: The Men's Study.*

After writing the men's study, my husband joined SaveOne full-time, and Jack then rewrote the men's study from a man's viewpoint. He made it ten times better, and we have had a hard time keeping it on the shelf.

No! Abortion is not just about women. An aborted child was just as much *his* as it was *hers*.

After the men's study, I then wrote *SaveOne: The Ripple Effect*. I wrote the third book for friends and loved ones who grieve an abortion decision by someone close to them. All three of these studies complement each other, so all three can be used in the same class.

SaveOne has continued to grow over the years. And as of this writing, we have established 280 chapters (pregnancy centers and churches teaching our studies) in 23 countries. The growth of SaveOne certainly testifies to the size of the need.

SaveOne has joined many others in battling against the deception of proponents of abortion, and we believe we are seeing abortion end in our country and around the world through the stories people who are healed are now able to tell.

The women, men, and families who have experienced abortion are the greatest voices to be telling the truth of what abortion truly does to people. Thanks to the leaders in pregnancy centers and churches, who are on the front lines of this issue, we are seeing people set free, lives transformed, both women and men accepting Jesus as their Savior, marriages restored, families reconciled, generational curses broken, and abortions cancelled.

God has walked me through forgiving the abusers in my life and owning my bad choices. He has wiped my slate clean and made me a victor over my past circumstances. I am no longer a victim. What happened to me as a child is not what defines me. And God has used all of my experiences in life to strengthen me and prepare me for my work today.

The enemy meant all that junk for nothing but destruction in my life, but God used it all for my betterment and that of my awesome family. He has increased my abilities to help others who are going through the same type of situations I experienced.

It is my passion and purpose to go wherever, speak to whomever, and do whatever it takes to get the job done. "What is that job?" you ask? To see abortion end in our country and around our world.

So there's my story. I know that without God's grace I would still be a mess, true and simple. But with His grace, life is awesome.

—Sheila Harper, Founder/President, SaveOne[21]

---

21 You can get more information about Sheila's work at her web site: *https://saveone.org*. And if you are interested in starting a SaveOne chapter near you, please fill out the inquiry on the web site, or send an e-mail message to *info@saveone.org* to start the process. There is no required fee for starting a SaveOne chapter, and the leaders of the SaveOne organization provide free resources to local chapters as they focus on making it as easy as possible for local chapters to excel in helping others.

As you can see, God has brought beauty from ashes in the lives of both Sherry and Sheila. And through their powerful personal testimonies God is continuing to repair the damage the enemy is doing through his deceptive influences concerning abortion.

The world would have women believe it is their *right* to do as they please with their bodies—even if that means terminating another life growing within their own wombs. However, as Sheila made clear, fathers also have a serious interest in their decisions. But beyond the rights of the fathers of the babies growing within their mothers' wombs, what about the babies' rights?

And what about God's rights?

Who will speak out for the rights of the child? And who will speak out on behalf of God as He attempts to bring people to himself in personal, healing relationships? He is doing that to impart to them both the wisdom they need to avoid deception and the restoration they need for the results of what yielding to deception brought into their lives.

We must speak truth and take the mask off of every deceptive falsehood. The masquerade must end. Abortion is not a right. Abortion is not an expression of a compassionate society. Abortion is wrong. Abortion is death.

And as I stated at the beginning of this chapter, babies are not the only ones dying. Those who choose death over life for their babies are more likely to end up seeking their own deaths in response to their decisions.

Choosing abortion is a deadly decision in every way. We must do everything we can to prevent people from being deceived by the lies and perceived justifications given for making that choice. At the same time, we must speak in love and tenderly minister to those who are already suffering from the aftermath of that tragic decision.

We can, *and must*, do both.

Perhaps you will be faced with the temptation to abort your child. Perhaps you are facing that temptation right now! Know this: the idea that abortion is a solution to your problems is a terrible deception. It will only bring death to your child and sorrow to your own life.

Turn to God and seek out people who will truly help you know and follow truth and avoid deception not only now but throughout your life. They want to help you.

Perhaps you yourself have already had an abortion. I want you to know there is hope for your future because there is forgiveness for you now, and the forgiveness you ultimately need is found only in Jesus. Only He can forgive sins, heal you of the effects of past decisions, and restore you to spiritual and emotional wholeness.

I encourage you to seek godly counsel and move forward into the wonderful life I know God has planned for you.

DISCUSSION QUESTIONS

1. Abortion has become so common in our day that most all of us know someone who has been impacted by it. What would you tell a young lady who has been convinced that abortion is completely normal and acceptable?

2. Write the Bible verse, Psalm 127:3, on the lines below. What does it tell us about children?

_____

_____

_____

_____

_____

3. Can you think of other ways the enemy has attempted to deceive us by causing us to believe our personal rights are more important than God's truth?

_____

_____

_____

_____

4. What does 1 Peter 5:8 tell us about our enemy? How is this Scripture made clear through the deception surrounding abortion?

_____

_____

_____

_____

CHAPTER 6

IGNORING THE SIGNS

ONE OF THE most bizarre events in history occurred on Boston's North End shortly after noon on January 15, 1919. That event became known as the Great Molasses Flood.[22] A giant storage tank burst open, and out of the ruptured tank spilled more than two million gallons of thick, brown molasses.

The enormous tank of molasses, whose contents were used for distilling alcohol, measured fifty feet tall and ninety feet in diameter. And when it split apart the results were immediate and powerful as it produced a very sticky tsunami ranging up to twenty-five feet high and reaching an estimated speed of thirty-five miles per hour.

It may sound like something out of a comic book or a cartoon, but it was definitely no laughing matter when it happened. The molasses swept away people, horses, and pets as it poured into

---

22 https://en.wikipedia.org/wiki/Great_Molasses_Flood;
https://www.history.com/news/the-great-molasses-flood-of-1919

and flooded an area the size of several city blocks. The wave of sweet-smelling molasses crushed buildings and killed at least twenty-one people while injuring one hundred-fifty more.

After an investigation it was determined that the failure of the tank was the result of a combination of bad engineering, faulty materials, poor construction, and improper safety tests during construction inspections.

But there is more to know.

The failure didn't just happen overnight—that is, without warning. The operators of the facility—Purity Distilling—knew about the creaking and groaning of the tank every time it was filled. And they knew about cracks that had appeared in the tank. The company's response was to caulk the cracks. But the tank continued to leak so badly and so often that the company actually painted the tank brown to help disguise the warning signs.

The company ignored the seriousness of the tank's problems, but they weren't the only ones who knew about the tank's issues. All the people who lived or worked around the facility heard the noises made by the tank when it was filled. And the leaks were so well known by Bostonians that people would take cups to the tank and collect molasses leaking from the cracks to use at home.

Everyone knew the tank had issues, and those issues were signs pointing to the future collapse of the tank, but no one responded properly to the giant tank's warning signs as it loomed in ominous distress over the city. People assumed the tank would continue to stand, and the next day would be like the last. They couldn't imagine what was coming to suddenly disrupt their lives.

On January 14 a ship arrived in the harbor with a new delivery of molasses. The tank was filled again, and I'm sure the tank groaned and creaked again just like during other fillings. Once again the company officials and the people in the area no doubt heard the sound, but it was no different from other days when the tank was filled. They had no idea the tank would collapse the next day. And when it did, they were caught unprepared.

Ignoring the troubling signs and continuing to live like that tank would stand forever was a huge mistake.

When I found out about the story of the Great Molasses Flood, I couldn't help but think about what the Bible says about Jesus' future return, about the signs of His coming, and about people being unprepared for it.

Just as the people in Boston saw and heard the troubling signs before the tank collapsed but were unprepared for the results, many people see the signs pointing to Christ's return but will be unprepared for that too. But even more tragic, on the very day when Jesus returns many people will not just be ignoring the signs themselves; sadly, they will be encouraging others to ignore them too.

In these last days, like the company painting the molasses tank to hide the evidence pointing to future disaster, the enemies of truth are glossing over and trying to disguise or discount the signs pointing to our Lord's return. But no hiding or explaining away the signs will keep the Lord from fulfilling His promises.

Before dealing more fully with the return of Christ and the deceptiveness of the falsehoods being spread about it by Satan and the enemies of the Church, it's best to understand some things about the end-time events prophesied in the Bible. I won't go into a lot of detail about Bible prophecy since actually studying that is not part of my purpose, but I'll establish a little about the order of future things foretold in the Bible.

When it comes to understanding or explaining how end-time events and the timing of Christ's return unfold, one of the major views held by people who study Bible prophecy is called *premillennialism*. I am a *premillennialist*. That is, I believe in premillennialism, in which the major divisions or events of the end times can be listed in the following chronological order:

- The Sudden Rapture of the Church
- The Period of Great Tribulation—immediately following the Rapture
- The Physical Second Coming of Christ—at the end of the Tribulation
- The Millennial Reign of Christ on Earth—a thousand years of peace
- The Final Day of Judgment—at the end of the Millennium

At the Rapture, Jesus will suddenly appear in the air above the earth; the dead in Christ will be resurrected; and together with the believers still living they will be caught up in the air to meet Christ and be taken to heaven.[23]

After the rapture, the antichrist and false prophet will then be revealed, and a period of great tribulation and trouble will follow as God pours out His wrath on the earth.

At the end of that time of tribulation, Jesus will return again to live on earth—to physically rule and reign among mankind during a thousand years of peace. And when the Lord comes then to reign, He will bring with Him those who were taken up in the Rapture, and they will rule and reign with Him.[24]

Then following that Millennial Reign of Christ, everyone still in the graves—those who didn't take part in the first resurrection

---

23 1 Thessalonians 4:15-17; Revelation 20:5-6.

24 "Blessed and holy are those who share in the first resurrection. For them the second death holds no power, but they will be priests of God and of Christ and will reign with him a thousand years" (Revelation 20:6).

(during the Rapture)—will be resurrected to face the final Day of Judgment.[25]

The Bible doesn't tell us specifically when Jesus will return. But here is some of what Jesus had to say about it as recorded by Matthew:

> But about that day or hour no one knows, not even the angels in heaven, nor the Son, but only the Father. As it was in the days of Noah, so it will be at the coming of the Son of Man. For in the days before the flood, people were eating and drinking, marrying and giving in marriage, up to the day Noah entered the ark; and they knew nothing about what would happen until the flood came and took them all away. That is how it will be at the coming of the Son of Man. (Matthew 24:36-39 NIV)

While speaking of His return, Jesus made it clear that just as the people in Noah's day were simply going about their business like they had no concern in the world while Noah was building the ark and warning people of the judgment to come,[26] people will be doing the same when He returns.

Today, many have either grown complacent or are in complete denial about the fact that Jesus is coming again. They've heard the warnings. They see the signs prophesied in Scripture. But they constantly ignore them. But even more troubling, many people actually scoff at the idea of the Lord's return.

However, without realizing it, their own words of denial and disbelief are actually fulfilling Bible prophecy. This is what Peter had to say about the last days:

---

25 Revelation 20:11-13.

26 "And God did not spare the ancient world—except for Noah and the seven others in his family. Noah warned the world of God's righteous judgment. So God protected Noah when he destroyed the world of ungodly people with a vast flood" (2 Peter 2:5).

Most importantly, I want to remind you that in the last days scoffers will come, mocking the truth and following their own desires. They will say, "What happened to the promise that Jesus is coming again? From before the times of our ancestors, everything has remained the same since the world was first created."

(2 Peter 3:3-4)

I had someone very close to me tell me she no longer believed Jesus is coming again. And she was not only someone I went to church with but also one who taught me the Scriptures as a child.

I could not believe that my friend and former Bible teacher could possibly come to believe that Jesus will not return for His Church. But she actually gave me the classic response used by all too many. She said she had heard all her life that Jesus could come any second, and He hasn't returned.

She had lost faith and given up, and that broke my heart.

We know that some believers will fall away in the last days before Christ returns.[27] And some of them will do it because they become disappointed by what they view as Christ's failure to fulfill His promise to return. But that does not change the fact that Jesus is coming back.

There is actually a biblical reason for the Lord delaying His return, and Peter wrote about it.

But you must not forget this one thing, dear friends: A day is like a thousand years to the Lord, and a thousand years is like a day. The Lord isn't really being slow about his promise, as some people think. No, he is being patient for your sake. He does not want anyone to be destroyed, but wants everyone to repent.

(2 Peter 3:8-9)

---

27 "Now the Holy Spirit tells us clearly that in the last times some will turn away from the true faith; they will follow deceptive spirits and teachings that come from demons" (1 Timothy 4:1).

Don't believe anyone who tells you Jesus is not coming back. God doesn't lie. The Scriptures don't lie. The truth will stand forever. Jesus is coming again, and He hasn't come back yet because He loves people and demonstrates a patience greater than you and I could ever understand.

The first part of the Lord's return—the Rapture of the Church—will be a turning point in history. It will be a time of victory for those who are caught up to be with the Lord in the air. But it will also introduce a terrible time of trouble on earth and point toward the coming judgments of God.

I won't go into detail about all the ways the world will change or how God will pour out His wrath after the Rapture, but suffice it to say the following years won't be pleasant. You can read about it in the book of Revelation.

We may view today as full of trouble, hate, war, disasters, and death, but it is nothing compared to what it will be like during the tribulation period. And the approaching Day of Judgment and eternal punishment of the wicked will be even worse than the death and destruction facing the earth during the Tribulation.

The Bible teaches us that after the Tribulation, and following the millennial reign of Christ on earth, the devil will once again cause trouble and attempt to deceive the nations.[28] Once again his lies and deception will result in people yielding to his masquerade as he once again rises up in opposition to God.

But the Lord will make short work of that. And God will put a final end to deception and the sin, trouble, and strife it causes.

---

28 Revelation 20:1-3, 7-8.

Satan will be cast into the lake of fire that burns forever and ever.[29] Then will come the Day of Judgment.

Chapter twenty-four and chapter twenty-five of Matthew contain a record of Jesus' teaching concerning the future, His return, and the final judgment. In chapter twenty-five we read that Jesus used two parables to illustrate His lesson—the parable of ten bridesmaids and the parable of the three servants. Then He summarized His message by saying precisely what is going to happen when He judges the world on that day.

Among His closing points were these:

> *But when the Son of Man* [**Jesus**] *comes in his glory* [**His return to earth**], *and all the angels with him, then he will sit upon his glorious throne. All the nations will be gathered in his presence, and he will separate the people as a shepherd separates the sheep from the goats. He will place the sheep at his right hand and the goats at his left.*
>
> *Then the King will say to those on his right, "Come, you who are blessed by my Father, inherit the Kingdom prepared for you from the creation of the world."*
>
> *. . .*
>
> *Then the King will turn to those on the left and say, "Away with you, you cursed ones, into the eternal fire prepared for the devil and his demons."*   (Matthew 25:31-41 [emphasis mine])

---

29 "When the thousand years come to an end, Satan will be let out of his prison. He will go out to deceive the nations—called Gog and Magog—in every corner of the earth. He will gather them together for battle—a mighty army, as numberless as sand along the seashore. And I saw them as they went up on the broad plain of the earth and surrounded God's people and the beloved city. But fire from heaven came down on the attacking armies and consumed them. Then the devil, who had deceived them, was thrown into the fiery lake of burning sulfur, joining the beast and the false prophet. There they will be tormented day and night forever and ever" (Revelation 20:7-10).

The final place of punishment—the lake of eternal fire—was not made for people. It was prepared for Satan and his demons. But because our God is a God of justice, there must be a punishment for rejecting Christ and living a life of sin.

So those who are refusing to follow Christ on that day—the goats—and all those who died throughout history while refusing to follow Christ, will ultimately be cast into the lake of fire with the devil and his demons.

Many people say that *a loving God* would never send people to hell. But as you can see in the verses quoted above, Jesus said they are wrong.

But I will agree with them only in one way; for God gives us the right to make decisions about our eternal future when we choose to either accept or deny Christ. So looking at it from that perspective, in a real sense people who reject Christ are actually choosing judgment for themselves.

Jesus offers to us His precious gift of salvation, but the choice of accepting it is ours. God is merciful, so God waits patiently—hoping more and more people will turn from their sins and accept His offer to save them from eternity in the lake of fire. But although God himself is the ultimate expression of love,[30] it is only He who will be the judge on the Day of Judgment.

Don't deceive yourself into believing the lies that demote God into a position of having to see things like we may want them to be. And don't be convinced that what the Bible predicts about the future will turn out any other way than how the Scriptures promise.

God's Word does not change, and God fulfills all His promises. If the Bible says Jesus is coming again to take Christians out of this world, then you can take that to the bank!

---

30 "But anyone who does not love does not know God, for God is love" (1 John 4:8).

One day Jesus *will* come and snatch away believers along with all the believers who died through the ages.[31] He *will* then come again to rule and reign for a thousand years. And finally, He *will* judge both the living and the dead on the Day of Judgment.[32]

Don't let the devil or anyone who follows his deceptions convince you otherwise.

Judgment is coming. Prophecies in the Bible make that clear. But believers are expecting much more—*eternal life* instead of eternal punishment.

We're awaiting the Lord's return to take us out of the world before the years of the great tribulation, and long before the final Day of Judgment following the Millennial Reign. So as we move toward closing out this chapter let's move the focus back to the Rapture of the Church.

Paul wrote a letter to Titus, Paul's friend and partner in ministry. In that letter he called the Rapture of the Church *the blessed hope.* [33] It is indeed our blessed hope—our expectation and statement of faith—that Christ is coming back for us. But the Thessalonians were discouraged that believers among them were continuing to die, and the Lord had not yet returned. To them Paul wrote the following.

> *And now, dear brothers and sisters, we want you to know what will happen to the believers who have died so you will not grieve like people who have no hope. For since we believe that Jesus*

---

31 1 Thessalonians 4:16-17.

32 "Human pride will be brought down, and human arrogance will be humbled. Only the LORD will be exalted on that day of judgment" (Isaiah 2:11). I suggest a reading of the entire second chapter of Isaiah.

33 Titus 2:11-13 (KJV, NKJV, NIV, NASB).

died and was raised to life again, we also believe that when Jesus returns, God will bring back with him the believers who have died.

We tell you this directly from the Lord: We who are still living when the Lord returns will not meet him ahead of those who have died.

For the Lord himself will come down from heaven with a commanding shout, with the voice of the archangel, and with the trumpet call of God. First, the believers who have died will rise from their graves. Then, together with them, we who are still alive and remain on the earth will be caught up in the clouds to meet the Lord in the air. Then we will be with the Lord forever. So encourage each other with these words.

(1 Thessalonians 4:13-18)

And to the church in Corinth, Paul wrote:

But let me reveal to you a wonderful secret. We will not all die, but we will all be transformed! It will happen in a moment, in the blink of an eye, when the last trumpet is blown. For when the trumpet sounds, those who have died will be raised to live forever. And we who are living will also be transformed. For our dying bodies must be transformed into bodies that will never die; our mortal bodies must be transformed into immortal bodies."

(1 Corinthians 15:51-53)

And quoting again from Matthew, following the words of Christ when He likened the day of His return to the days of Noah, Jesus continued by saying:

Two men will be working together in the field; one will be taken, the other left. Two women will be grinding flour at the mill; one will be taken, the other left. So you, too, must keep watch! For you don't know what day your Lord is coming.

(Matthew 24:40-42)

The Scriptures above speak of the first reappearance of Christ in the air, not to the day when He returns to establish an earthly kingdom. These are encouraging words about the sudden, first return of Christ in the last days—the Rapture—and that can happen any day of our heavenly Father's choosing.

To those who are not believers, the return of Christ—the Rapture—is a very scary thought. To be left behind when saved loved ones, children, and friends are taken away to be with Jesus will be terrifying.

And perhaps the thought of that alone is why many want to dismiss the idea of the Rapture entirely. But regardless of their own motivations, the enemy continues to do everything he can to propagate the lie that Jesus is not coming again.

Satan and those in agreement with him have used every deceptive way of reasoning that mankind has been able to come up with to sow seeds of doubt and get people to accept any excuse to deny the truth of Christ's imminent return. They have done everything they can to convince the world that it is just a fairy tale.

But the truth still stands. Jesus is coming again, and we must be ready.

The prospect of Christ's return should not be a scary thought for the believer. We don't have anything to fear. Perhaps you remember some of these words from the old song by Alfred E. Brumley:

This world is not my home, I'm just a passing through
My treasures are laid up somewhere beyond the blue;
The angels beckon me from heaven's open door,
And I can't feel at home in this world anymore.

We should be excited by the prospect of *going home* to be with our Lord.

We should anticipate the day God calls us home. I personally cannot wait to meet the One who laid down His life for me. I can't imagine anything sweeter.

But because of the Rapture's association with other end-time events, it is no wonder that so many people want to ignore the Lord's return for the Church. For while the Rapture means salvation to the saved, it reminds the lost of impending, future judgment.

The return of Christ and the judgment to follow is not a popular topic. That is why so many have backed away from preaching about it. But how will people heed the warnings if no one is doing the warning? We must point out the signs to others and not allow them to be covered up—hidden from view by deceptive means.

God is patient. But one good look at the world we are living in today should cause us to wonder *how much longer* God's patience will last. Some may read this and say, "Oh, you are just resorting to fear tactics now!" No, I'm resorting to *truth tactics*, and if the truth scares us, there are surely things in our lives that need to change.

We simply cannot be silent now. Too many lives are at stake. Jesus is coming again, and we must remove the enemy's mask as he attempts to deceive people into thinking all is well.

Satan and the enemies of God are patching up and painting over the signs of the times, and they are doing everything they can to close up the ears of people living today so they will not hear the groaning and creaking of a great tank of spiritual darkness looming over them—a tank that will one day explode and violently pour out its contents upon the earth following the Rapture.

Let's do our best to defeat the lies of the enemy, reveal his deceptions, and continually point people to the truth of Christ's soon return and the judgments coming in the future. We have a lot of work to do, and the time is short.

And as we go about helping others avoid complacency about the future, let's make sure we ourselves refuse to be deafened and blinded to the signs pointing to what is about to happen.

However, no one knows the day or hour when these things will happen, not even the angels in heaven or the Son himself. Only the Father knows. And since you don't know when that time will come, be on guard! Stay alert!" (Mark 13:32-33)

DISCUSSION QUESTIONS

1. Did you know the New Testament refers to the return of Christ more than three hundred times? Write the words of Acts 1:11 on the lines below. What does the first chapter of Acts tell us about Christ's return?

---

2. Who will rise first when Jesus returns according to Paul's first letter to the Thessalonians?

---

3. Why do you think Satan desires to deceive people about the imminent return of Christ?

_____

_____

_____

_____

_____

_____

4. What are some of the arguments you have heard from non-believers about the return of Christ?

_____

_____

_____

_____

_____

5. According to the third chapter of Second Peter (2 Peter), what should we do to speed the day of the Lord's return?

_____

_____

_____

_____

_____

CHAPTER 7

DECEIVED WORTH

ONE OF THE hardest things I have had to overcome in my life is being deceived about my worth—feeling like I am unworthy. After so many years of talking with others, I think most if not all of us have at some time or another struggled with that. And realizing our worth—especially our value to God—can be a particularly difficult challenge when we are dealing with past mistakes or failures.

I shared much of my testimony and many of my struggles with failure in my first book, *Beauty from Ashes: My Story of Grace*, so I won't share my whole story again in this book. But, I will give you a glimpse into my past here so you will better understand why I feel Satan works to perpetuate feelings of worthlessness in our lives.

I was divorced twice by the age of twenty-three, and because of those experiences I struggled with the fear of abandonment and a low self-image. *I felt like something was wrong with me.* I was raised in a Christian home and lived as a Christian up until that point. But because of my disappointment, anger, and lack of self-respect I soon turned to drugs and alcohol, which served to only compound my problems.

I became extremely depressed to the point of becoming suicidal well into my third marriage. Deep down I believed that my husband, Bryan, would leave me as soon as he realized there was something wrong with me. And I was certain it was only a matter of time.

God never gave up on me, though, and eventually the Holy Spirit got my attention. I finally repented and surrendered my life to Christ. Then Bryan also came to know Jesus as Savior. Soon we had two beautiful daughters, and then God moved us from Tennessee to Iowa. (I went kicking and screaming.)

We were soon settled into a new church, and I began to feel a tug toward ministry. However, as powerful as that tug felt, I equally felt the shame and guilt of not measuring up. I was still haunted by the guilt of previously turning my back on God and choosing a life of sin. After all, I had been raised in church. I knew better, but I had done it anyway.

I was sure God had forgiven me, because I had repented and turned from my sins, but I was also pretty sure He was still angry with me—or at least still very disappointed in me. So as I looked at things back then, I felt it was in my best interest to keep quiet and try to remain unnoticed *in the crowd.*

"For surely," I thought, "if anyone learns about my failures or anything about my past marriages they will not want to be with me."

But still, the desire to be involved in ministry continued to grow inside my heart. I began to envision myself preaching, although I never spoke a word about it to anyone.

"How crazy would that be?" I considered.

I saw myself as a loser.

"Me telling others how they should live their lives for Christ with a myriad of mistakes and failures in my past? What a joke! That could never happen. God could never use someone like me."

I felt totally worthless when it came to contributing to God's kingdom.

Every time the thought of being involved in any kind of ministry came to mind I would dismiss it. After all, the enemy and his influences made sure I had plenty of guilty reminders to discourage such a crazy idea. I simply could not see myself having any worth to Christ. I felt I had long ago messed up any plans the Lord might have had for me.

As I continued to struggle with the idea of doing anything significant for God, the enemy's influence continued to keep me focused on my past mistakes. There was a spiritual battle taking place, but I was completely unaware of it.

One night a visiting pastor spoke at our small church, and I went to the altar for prayer after his sermon. I honestly can't remember what kind of invitation he gave that night. But I will never forget the moment he stopped in front of me and said, "Ma'am God has called you to be an evangelist!"

I looked at him with my heart racing. Oh, how I wished that could be true!

But it just couldn't be possible. "If he only knew about my past, he would feel very silly for saying that God has called me to do these things," I mused.

The excitement of hearing his words faded in the days to come as I continued to embrace the lie that persuaded me to believe I remained unworthy before God. But I never forgot that preacher's words.

I was stuck believing that God was angry with me. And I felt I deserved His feelings. That was part of the enemy's deception, and because I accepted it, I felt a separation between me and God. There was such a heaviness, such a feeling that *I blew it*, that I just couldn't shake the deception I was under.

As I think back on it now—having of course lived through it, and after having been delivered from that deception—I'm amazed how I could accept God's forgiveness but not accept the fullness of His love.

But now, fast forward a couple of years to a women's conference I attended with the ladies from my church.

None of the ladies knew my story. I was secretive about my past because I feared what they would think of me if they knew about it. I was certain they would reject me if they knew, and if that happened it would only serve to reinforce my lack of self-esteem.

At that point, though, I was at an impasse in my life. I felt my relationship with Christ was going nowhere, and I couldn't stand the feeling of being stagnant. I decided it was time to either go-all-in or quit trying to convince myself that I was even a Christian.

I was miserably restless. I couldn't understand that I was experiencing the weariness of a battle. It is so tiring to fight a true calling to ministry—especially when allowing mistakes and failures of the past to haunt and deceive us into unhealthy and false assessments of our value to God.

I simply could not put out of my mind the desire and *hope* that maybe, just maybe, God could actually still use me in spite of my past life. But I continued to deny myself the full truth that God's love and forgiveness was complete and God not only *could* use me but also *wanted* to use me. And that constant mental battle was absolutely exhausting.

The battle had to end—one way or another.

I'm so glad God sees us as **what we can be** instead of **what we are or were**. And I'm glad God knows how to lead us to the solutions He has for our problems.

The Lord knew exactly what He was doing when He led me to that women's conference. As we began to sing, and as tears rolled down my cheeks, I quietly prayed and told God that if there was anything at all He could do with my life, I wanted to give it all away—to Him—to use.

Something happens when we finally and fully surrender to God. When we take just a moment to silence the lies, that's the moment our chains fall to the ground with a clunk! And as my chains fell that night, something amazing happened. God's love and His assurance of how much I was worth to Him flowed into me.

I began to realize that although others may never see my true worth as a person seeking His will in my life, God always will. I was completely overwhelmed with the warmth and intensity of His love! Every deceptive thought instigated by the enemy lost all power and influence over me. And as I wept like a baby before God, the Lord began to reconstruct my faulty thought process.

In the following months God began to show me that using my mistakes and failures would actually soon become one of my greatest ministry tools. The very things I had tried to bury and hide would soon be on display for others to see and learn from— not because I was proud of them, but because God was using my story to rescue others *through* them.

When our thoughts are taken captive and reconditioned by the love of Jesus, we can finally see past the lies of the enemy. We can truly understand who we are in Christ.

If we allow God to let us see things through His eyes, we begin to see things from a completely different perspective. We suddenly realize we have always been—and continue to be—worth more to Him than we ever knew.

Never, ever, forget this: Jesus paid the ultimate price for our forgiveness because God decided we were worth it!

> *When we were utterly helpless, Christ came at just the right time and died for us sinners. Now, most people would not be willing to die for an upright person, though someone might perhaps be willing to die for a person who is especially good. But God showed his great love for us by sending Christ to die for us while we were still sinners.* (Romans 5:6-8)

God didn't wait for us to prove ourselves or even ask Him for salvation before He acted to prove our value to Him. Does that sound like He is someone who would ever want us to be bound by our failures and blind to our worth?

If Jesus was willing to die for us on the Cross in spite of all the sins we would commit in the future, and in spite of all our future failures (which He certainly foresaw), it is illogical for any of us to believe that He would ever want us to feel unworthy of His love and value in His kingdom.

But Satan uses all of the resources at his disposal to blind people to God's amazing love. And he certainly doesn't want people to see God's intentions to call them and use them despite their failures and weaknesses. The devil wants to continually deceive people and blind them to how God views us. He wants to make us see ourselves as unworthy of God's love and unfit to represent the Lord in any way.

You and I are involved in a spiritual battle.

> *Be strong in the Lord and in his mighty power. Put on all of God's armor so that you will be able to stand firm against all strategies of the devil. For we are not fighting against flesh-and-blood enemies, but against evil rulers and authorities of the unseen*

*world, against mighty powers in this dark world, and against evil
spirits in the heavenly places.*   (Ephesians 6:10b–12)

The evil powers and lying spirits at work in our world are
ruled and manipulated by Satan, and they are doing everything
they can to separate us from God. They are at the forefront of
misrepresenting truth. All the evil influences in this world are
working to keep you from fully understanding God's love for you.

And the unredeemed world has yielded itself to Satan's
masquerade. So when the world and its influences appear to be
your friend, don't be fooled. It's all a charade. Even when the
influences of the world appear to acknowledge or exalt God,
if they are at the same time holding you captive to shame and
reproach for past failures, you must recognize the masks they
wear, reject their efforts, and battle against them.

*Therefore, put on every piece of God's armor so you will be able to
resist the enemy in the time of evil. Then after the battle you will
still be standing firm. Stand your ground, putting on the belt of
truth and the body armor of God's righteousness. For shoes, put on
the peace that comes from the Good News so that you will be fully
prepared. In addition to all of these, hold up the shield of faith to
stop the fiery arrows of the devil. Put on salvation as your helmet,
and take the sword of the Spirit, which is the word of God.*

(Ephesians 6:13-17)

We must not be fooled by any lies propagated by the enemy,
the world, and their influences. We must stand our ground
against them. We must stand in faith. We must accept and trust
what the Word of God says and use it as our weapon to defeat
deception and falsehood.

The Bible teaches us the truth. Christ died so we can be
forgiven of our sins and failures. And He wants us to be *completely*
free from them. He doesn't want them to hold us back from doing

His will. After we repent of our failures and accept the forgiveness the Lord so freely offers us, He wants us to leave them in the past and continue our march into the future under His leadership.

If we will do that, God will honor our faith. He will reinforce to us His own opinion of our value—which matters most. He will prove to us over and over that the past cannot defeat or limit us because it cannot defeat or limit Him.[34] And with a healthy, balanced understanding of both His worth and ours, we will go forward to win victory after victory in His name.

When it comes to getting people to understand and accept their true value to God, the deceptions the enemy uses against them have sometimes been terribly frustrating for me. They frustrate me because I so often see the results of people accepting the devil's lies.

I continually deal with people bound up in their own struggles to have a healthy self-image. And I am especially aware of it as I go into the jails to minister to prisoners.

I've seen many women in jail accept Christ. And I've seen them delivered from years of feeling their lives were worthless. But not all of the women to whom I minister become free from the lies promoted to them by others—or by themselves.

I've seen women saved and elevated to having healthy, God-centered views of themselves even though they are still behind bars in jail. But I've seen others who were still bound by spiritual bars of self-loathing even after being released from prison.

When people accept the lie that their lives are worthless, they can believe their lives are destined to consist of never-ending

---

34 There truly are no limits to what God can do for us and with us when we simply yield to Him in faith. For more on this topic read Donna's book, *No Limits: Embracing the Miraculous*—[Editor].

cycles of perpetual failures. They can come to feel like prisoners given a life sentence of loathing themselves with no chance of escape. And unfortunately, all too many of them at that point accept their feeling as God's truth and just give up trying to see things differently.

We must reject the devil's deceptions, and the world's lies, and not live like spiritual prisoners!

I pause here to say that despite all of God's efforts and revelations to us, and despite the biblical, inspired messages we receive or deliver to others about God's love and promises of restoration, acceptance of the truth comes down to personal decisions. Each of us will decide for himself or herself to either yield to God's truths or continue to live in deception.

What will you decide?

Looking back at my own life, I can see how the enemy's influence on my thoughts would have benefitted his purposes had I continued to yield to his deceptions. If I had given up to them I might not have guided my daughters into a relationship with Christ. And if I had given up I certainly wouldn't be involved today in evangelistic ministry.

Clearly, if I had given up to the deception of seeing myself as worthless, not only would I still be living a miserable life but I would also still be contributing to the misery of others.

If I had continued to see myself as worthless to God, the *evil rulers and authorities of the unseen world*, the *mighty powers in this dark world*, and the *evil spirits in the heavenly places* would still be rejoicing over it today. And for sure—if you give up to self-loathing, continue focusing on your failures, and allow a feeling of worthlessness to determine your future, all of them will rejoice over your decision too.

I know if I had not accepted God's view of me I very well could have continued to struggle with the terrible depression that had me bound and limited for so long. And by continuing to seek personal affirmation or validation from others instead of finding them in Christ's actions and God's Word, the deception I was under could have led me into sins that would have destroyed my marriage, my life, and especially my ministry.

But God got through to me. I allowed the Holy Spirit to reveal to me that my past is absolutely in the past, and my future is in the hands of my loving Savior. You see, everything changes when we experience the Savior's love. His love is greater and stronger than any influence on earth, and it is ready for us to accept.

That is why the enemy tries so desperately to keep us from encountering God's love and compassion. If Satan and his helpers in the world can perpetuate the lie that we are not worthy of God's love, or that God is angry or disappointed with us even after He forgives us, then they can keep us under a cloud of condemnation where we feel too inadequate or ashamed to approach God.

I am reminded of the story in the book of John about Jesus meeting the woman at the well. She was a woman who had multiple failed relationships in her past, and at the time she met Jesus she was living with a man who was not her husband.

I can only imagine the shame and condemnation she must have felt from the people in her village since they all knew about her life. Perhaps that is why she went to draw water at noon—in the heat of the day. Maybe she was trying to avoid the whispers and looks of disgust from other women who drew water from the well during cooler times of the day.

She was likely avoiding social interaction so she could stay in the background where she could hide from criticism. But Jesus sought her out. Even though no one else could see her worth, she was valuable to Him, and He was about to reveal that very thing to her in a way that was undeniable.

Jesus knew before He ever approached the well that the woman would be coming to draw water at that specific time. But the woman had no idea whom she would meet at the well that day or what was about to happen there. It was just an ordinary day for her. Yet her life was about to be completely altered. Her whole perception of herself was about to be turned upside down.

I can only assume that woman had long given up to Satan's deception that she could never be of any real value to God. And as she went to the well, I have a feeling she expected that day would finish up in the evening as just having been another day devoid of hope. But her day—and her life—was about to drastically change.

As she approached the well, she found Jesus there, and He asked her for a drink of water.

> *The woman was surprised, for Jews refuse to have anything to do with Samaritans. She said to Jesus, "You are a Jew, and I am a Samaritan woman. Why are you asking me for a drink?"*
>
> (John 4:9)

Instantly she knew there was something different about Jesus. He not only traveled through and stopped in Samaria—seen as a spiritually corrupt and defiling region avoided by self-respecting Jews (especially the spiritual leaders among them)—but He also spoke to a Samaritan woman. And she knew she was a woman who was guilty of many sins.

Then Jesus gave her a response she could not have imagined.

Jesus replied, "If you only knew the gift God has for you and who you are speaking to, you would ask me, and I would give you living water." (John 4:10)

I'm sure when that woman came into contact with the love of Jesus, she could see compassion revealed in His eyes as He spoke. He wasn't frowning on her with a look of disgust like she had grown so accustomed to from many others.

He spoke to her as if her life had value. And no doubt the tone of His voice and His very demeanor revealed kindness and concern for a woman whose life had up to then been a total disaster.

If you read the entire biblical narrative (John 4:1-42), you will see that from the very beginning Jesus had complete control of their conversation at the well—and all that followed. It was all planned. It was purposeful. And it was effective.

During the conversation (and jumping ahead in the story a bit), after Jesus purposely asked the woman to go get her husband—followed of course by her response that she didn't have a husband—the Lord let her know that He knew she'd had five husbands in the past, and she wasn't married to the man she was then living with. (vv. 16-18) She had failed in marriage many times. She was living in sin. And Jesus knew it.

To that, the woman then told Jesus, "*You must be a prophet,*" after which she immediately attempted to change the subject by redirecting the focus of the conversation from her failures and obvious needs to the issue of how Samaritans and the Jews differed on where people should worship. (vv. 19-20)

But with Jesus' response to that, He turned the conversation back to exactly where He wanted it to lead—to reveal to Her God's love and her true personal value to Him.

*The woman said, "I know the Messiah is coming—the one who is
called Christ. When he comes, he will explain everything to us."*

Then Jesus told her, "I AM the Messiah!"   (John 4:25-26)

Then Jesus' disciples—who had gone into town to get
supplies—returned to where Jesus was. When they saw Jesus
talking to the woman they questioned His activity in their hearts.

*Just then his disciples came back. They were shocked to find him
talking to a woman, but none of them had the nerve to ask, "What
do you want with her?" or "Why are you talking to her?"*

(John 4:27)

The feelings of the disciples were like those of others. The
woman was not worthy of the Lord's attention. He should not
have been speaking to such a worthless failure. It was simply not
done. It went contrary to what they had been taught about their
misguided spiritual responsibilities before God.

The woman left as the disciples returned. But the impact of
her encounter with what Jesus thought about her—and how it
differed from what the world around her thought of her—had
just begun to be understood.

*The woman left her water jar beside the well and ran back to
the village, telling everyone, "Come and see a man who told me
everything I ever did! Could he possibly be the Messiah?" So the
people came streaming from the village to see him.*

(John 4:28-30)

She couldn't keep it to herself. She was completely
overwhelmed by her encounter with Jesus. Because of what
she learned from Jesus that day—because of what Jesus revealed
to her—all of her thoughts of worthlessness dissipated as she

shamelessly ran into the town proclaiming the news about a man who had told her everything she had ever done.

Nothing will cause a person to proclaim Christ to the world like experiencing God's life-changing love and power.

After John recorded a short break in his narrative, in which he wrote about how Jesus used that event to teach His disciples more about the importance of His efforts of spreading the good news, he returned to the woman's story.

> *Many Samaritans from the village believed in Jesus because the woman had said, "He told me everything I ever did!" When they came out to see him, they begged him to stay in their village. So he stayed for two days, long enough for many more to hear his message and believe. Then they said to the woman, "Now we believe, not just because of what you told us, but because we have heard him ourselves. Now we know that he is indeed the Savior of the world."* (John 4:39-42)

The woman at the well became an evangelist that day as she heralded the news of the Messiah, whose short visit at the well turned into a two-day revival in their village. She met the Savior. She experienced His love. She accepted His message. And she knew the message of the Messiah included the complete removal of any barrier her past could place upon her future.

She may have never felt worthy to do anything of significance before, but when she saw herself through Jesus' eyes—and when she allowed Him to change and revolutionize how she thought of herself and her failures—she couldn't help but move from her state of being held back by shame into being a witness and worker in God's kingdom.

Oh, how the enemy wants us to remain in a state of deception when it comes to our worth in Christ! He would love for us to live in shame and feel defeated in every way. And if the enemy can use his influences to convince us we are incapable of achieving anything of value in our lives, he has won a great spiritual battle.

Understand your value to God and to His kingdom! Don't allow the enemy a victory in your life. Don't be held back by your past mistakes or even your failures tomorrow!

In closing, always remember that if the devil or any of his followers need to hide behind masks of religion to spread falsehoods about the fullness of God's love for us and our worth, they will do it. They will even pretend to speak for God to try to get you to believe that God himself wants you to continue to live in shame. But it's a lie.

They have no shame but want you to live in it every day. They will stop at nothing to stop you. And that's because our enemy and his followers are terrified of people who come to realize who they are in Jesus and begin to share His hope with the world.

If you are struggling with thoughts of worthlessness, please know that you are dearly loved by the One who created the heavens and the earth. And He wants to use *you* in His kingdom. That's my message for you. But more importantly that's the Bible's message for you. You can trust it.

God desires you to be totally free of any feelings that you are not worthy to come before Him, not worthy to enjoy your relationship with Him, or not worthy to work for Him.

If you are one of those who are bound by feelings of worthlessness, our wonderful Lord longs for you to draw close to Him so He can reconstruct your marred self-image. He wants to replace that disfigured self-image with the image *He* has of you. He sees you through eyes of love and compassion, and He desires to give you both a powerful hope and an active, joyful future.

Don't be deceived. Leave the past behind. Know and accept who you are and to whom you belong. Then act on it!

DISCUSSION QUESTIONS

1. What are some of the lies the enemy has used to cause you to think less of yourself than how God sees you?

2. Think of how you view others in your life. It seems we often see greater things in others than they can see in themselves. Do you know people who you could say really have no idea of their worth? What would you say to them?

3. Can you think of misconceptions you have about yourself that you have held on to but you know you should let go? What are they?

_____

_____

_____

_____

4. Do you have self-worth issues that have kept you from doing things for God? How has your perceptions of yourself held you back from offering God your very best?

_____

_____

_____

_____

_____

_____

5. Write the words of Psalms 139:13-14 below. How do these verses reveal our true worth?

_____

_____

_____

_____

_____

CHAPTER 8

DIVIDE AND CONQUER

TODAY IT SEEMS people are divided in many different ways. We are divided on worldwide issues, national issues, political issues, racial issues, moral and ethical issues, religious issues, and so much more. And sadly, the divisions trickle all the way down to invade our own family lives and affect our personal relationships.

As I began writing this book, I had no intention of composing a book that attempted to correct all the myriad views that divide us today. My intention was, and still is, to highlight truth and expose deception. But deception is something that causes division and conflict, so I hope by exposing deception we will be strengthened and brought together by what we have in common in Christ.

I am amazed by how groups of people with differing opinions and beliefs can drop their differences and come together in supporting one another when there is a tragedy such as a natural disaster or when a common enemy strikes. It seems that, for a moment in time, political views, personal preferences, racial tensions, and religious differences all fall by the wayside.

Our distrust, opposing views, opinions, and distaste for things—and even hatred—that separate us seem to dissolve and give way to sympathy, compassion, empathy, and support for our fellow man when we're confronted with a common enemy or challenge. For a brief period of time we recognize our frailty as human beings. And in those moments of fear and loss we find ourselves more focused on what connects us than on what separates us.

We are human. Our lives here on earth are fragile, and none of us are promised a tomorrow. Sometimes we just come together in recognizing that, and it's wonderful when that happens. But it never surprises me when, after some time has passed after the tragedy or challenge, people begin to pick up their same grudges and vengeful attitudes, and they fall back into their former routines that foster division.

How quickly we forget what binds us together!

Among all the things that should unify us and inspire us to action, one of the biggest things we have in common is something that is talked about in some circles far less than it should be. Some people may not even believe it's an issue worth addressing. But it is. It's a big issue, and hopefully what I've written in this book makes that clear.

We have a common spiritual adversary.

Knowing how to deal with our common adversary and his abilities to use our own inclinations toward selfishness and sin against us has been an issue that has existed from when man first walked on earth. Our common adversary, of course, is

Satan, and he is the original divider. While going about as usual, masquerading as an angel of light,[35] he constantly proves himself to be the originator of deception and division.

Satan is an antagonist and the enemy of our souls. And he has been dividing people from one another for a long time. He has been around long enough to know what tactics work best to accomplish that, and he has spent years perfecting them. And he is furiously going about in these last days doing everything he can to divide us, because he knows we are stronger together and weaker apart when standing against his plans for our destruction.

Though one may be overpowered, two can defend themselves. A cord of three strands is not quickly broken.

(Ecclesiastes 4:12 NIV)

Abraham Lincoln, who was soon to become the 16th President of the United States in 1860, knew the power of unity, and he used Scripture in his address at the Illinois State Capitol on June 16, 1858, to describe the dangers of division. He quoted a part of Scripture found in Matthew chapter twelve when he said, "A house divided against itself cannot stand."

And Jesus knew their thoughts, and said unto them, "Every kingdom divided against itself is brought to desolation; and every city or house divided against itself shall not stand."

(Matthew 12:25 KJV)

As I speak against division, I'm not saying it is wrong to have differing opinions or views. We will never completely agree on everything all the time. But when we see differences causing people to be filled with rage and hatred for others, those opinions and views have become too strong.

---

35 "Even Satan disguises himself as an angel of light" (2 Corinthians 11:14b). I have much more to say about the one who masquerades as an angel of light in Chapter 10, *The Counterfeit Angel of Light*.

And when we see people stop using meaningful discourse to try to convince others they are right and start exalting themselves into positions of power and seeking to destroy anyone or anything that disagrees with them, we absolutely must know there is something sinister feeding those differences that divide us.

We must be sure that we and others understand the devil is not only cheering on the rage and hatred that exists in the world today, he is actually behind much of it.

Division is Satan's specialty.

As time races on, societies change, issues change, and views change—for either the worse or the better. But two things are constant: Man is prone to pursuing self-interests, and therefore prone to temptation and sin,[36] and Satan is still the deceiver.[37] And those thoughts take me right to the earliest days of man.

In the book of Genesis we read how the serpent tempted Eve to sin. Satan was attempting to fool Eve in his first deceptive act to be recorded in Scripture.

> *One day he asked the woman, "Did God really say you must not eat the fruit from any of the trees in the garden?"*
>
> (Genesis 3:1b)

*"Did God **really** say . . .?"*[38]

The devil deceived Eve into questioning what God said. And the serpent's act of deception served his ultimate purpose. He was

---

36 "Temptation comes from our own desires, which entice us and drag us away" (James 1:14).

37 "Satan, who is the god of this world, has blinded the minds of those who don't believe" (2 Corinthians 4:4a).

38 I used Satan's deceptive words in Genesis 3:1 in chapter 4, *Even the Chosen*. It is such a powerful illustration that I use it again here to address *division*.

attempting to bring division between God and man. And because of the disobedience of Adam and Eve—because they ate the fruit God told them not to eat—Satan accomplished that.

And from that day to today, Satan has never stopped attempting to separate man from his Creator by deceiving people into questioning God's commands and rejecting His authority. And he continues to accomplish it over and over with many acts of deception and by using our fleshly desires and motivations against us.

But because of God's great love for us, He provided a way to heal the division that sin introduced into the world—to heal the division between God and man. God made a way for us to come back into fellowship with Him through the sacrifice of *"the Father's one and only Son,"* Jesus Christ.[39]

But in Satan's attempt to destroy God's intentions, he even tried his best to divide Jesus from the plan He and the Father drew up long before Jesus was born.[40] He tempted Jesus in the wilderness and tried everything he could to disrupt God's plan for our salvation through Christ.

But His perfect love for the Father—and for us—enabled Jesus to stand strong against Satan and his deceptive plans.[41] In his conquest for superiority and power, Satan tried his best to divide Jesus from God's plan, but he failed. Jesus was strong in His determination to accomplish God's will, and when Jesus resisted the devil, the devil had to flee from Him.[42]

39 John 1:14. Also read John 3:16, John 3:18, and 1 John 4:9.

40 How long ago did God draw up His plan for our salvation? In Revelation 13:8, John's words reveal Jesus as the "Lamb who was slaughtered before the world was made." That means God in His foreknowledge developed His plan for our salvation long before man was even tempted to sin— before man had even been made.

41 ". . . but I will do what the Father requires of me, so that the world will know that I love the Father" (John 14:31a).

42 "So humble yourselves before God. Resist the devil, and he will flee from you" (James 4:7).

When Satan came to tempt Jesus in the wilderness he used tactics like the ones he uses with us today.

First, he tempted Jesus by appealing to His *physical needs and desires.*

Jesus had been fasting for forty days. There is no doubt He was hungry. And Satan tempted Him to turn stones into bread. But Jesus denied himself and stood firm. And in doing so He denied not only His need and desire for food but also His own ability to go beyond human limitations to do whatever He decided to do. He was determined to do nothing that would affect His ability to fully identify with those whom He came to save.[43]

> *But Jesus told him "No! The Scriptures say, 'People do not live by bread alone, but by every word that comes from the mouth of God.'"*[44]   (Matthew 4:4)

Next, Satan tempted Jesus by appealing to His *identity*, or *ego*. He tempted Jesus to prove He was who He claimed to be (and who Satan knew He was). And in doing so, Satan further revealed his deceptive nature by quoting Scripture to add fuel to yet another temptation for Jesus to lay down His humanity and go beyond the limitations of His flesh—the limitations He intentionally took upon himself for us as part of God's plan.

---

43 One of the important keys to the success of God's plan was for Him to live among men, to experience fully man's weaknesses and temptation, and to become our Great High Priest, who can represent us and atone for our sins, in part, only because He understands our weaknesses. (Read Hebrews 2:17, 3:1, 4:14-16.) Jesus took upon himself the limitations of the flesh, and Satan was tempting Jesus to go beyond those limitations to turn stones into bread to satisfy His own needs and desires.

44 "Yes, he humbled you by letting you go hungry and then feeding you with manna, a food previously unknown to you and your ancestors. He did it to teach you that people do not live by bread alone; rather, we live by every word that comes from the mouth of the LORD" (Deuteronomy 8:3).

Then the devil took him to the holy city, Jerusalem, to the highest point of the Temple, and said, "If you are the Son of God, jump off! For the Scriptures say, 'He will order his angels to protect you. And they will hold you up with their hands so you won't even hurt your foot on a stone.'" (Matthew 4:5–6)

But Jesus refused to be divided from the Father's will and their united plan for our salvation, and once again Jesus stood against His enemy (and ours) by quoting the Word of God.

Jesus responded, "The Scriptures also say, 'You must not test the LORD your God.'" [45] (Matthew 4:7)

And finally, Satan tempted Jesus with the treasures of earth with all its kingdoms and splendor. He told Jesus if He would kneel down and worship him, he would give Jesus all those things. And again Jesus stood firm in His unity of purpose and commitment to the Father.

"Get out of here, Satan," Jesus told him. "For the Scriptures say, 'You must worship the LORD your God and serve only him.'" [46]
(Matthew 4:10)

We should not underestimate the pressure that was on Jesus during Satan's direct temptation of His flesh. It was real. And it was worse than any temptation you and I could imagine. Unlike you and me, Jesus could have easily turned stones into bread to satisfy His need for food during His fast (and long before Satan arrived to tempt Him). Jesus was not only fully man, He was fully God. He was God in the flesh—the God of miracles.

---

45 "You must not test the LORD your God as you did when you complained at Massah" (Deuteronomy 6:16).

46 "Then Samuel said to all the people of Israel, 'If you want to return to the LORD with all your hearts, get rid of your foreign gods and your images of Ashtoreth. Turn your hearts to the LORD and obey him alone . . .'" (1 Samuel 7:3).
"You must not have any other god but me" (Exodus 20:3).

He could have done what we couldn't do. And there was no sin Jesus would have committed by turning stones into bread. But He chose to stick with the plan.

And although Jesus could have easily proven His superiority over everyone in the world by having angels catch Him as He jumped from the highest point of the temple, He refused to take advantage of His full identity and chose to remain in His place in God's plan.

Then, we know Jesus lived a meager, humble life. The appeal to gain what the world offered to satisfy and exalt His flesh— the appeal to end His confinement to a life of lack and suffering within God's plan—was beyond real.

But Jesus once again stood strong and determined in the face of temptation. And because Jesus knew that yielding to the third temptation would not only put an end to the plan for our salvation but also disrupt the entire heavenly order, He refused to yield to Satan's deceptive attack on Him.

Jesus stood in unity with the Father and in agreement with their plan for our salvation. He did not let the enemy separate Him from God's plan for His life and eventual death on the Cross. And we must not allow temptation—whether it comes from the everyday desires of our own flesh or the enemy's direct acts of deception—divide us from God or His purposes in our lives.

Some methods Satan has always used to lure people into making bad decisions that in turn cause division among people, and between people and God, can be seen in the ways he tempted Jesus.

SATAN APPEALS TO PHYSICAL NEEDS
AND DESIRES TO DIVIDE US

God made us to be like Him—that is, to be a reflection of Him and possess a spirit that is meant to live forever in fellowship with Him. But just as it was in the beginning, we live in a body of flesh. And that flesh has needs and desires.

God made us to have needs. And those needs actually go beyond a need for physical sustenance. We also have needs related to spiritual nourishment—like needs for feeling loved, respected, and valued.

God also made us to have a normal, healthy desire for our needs to be met. And as we go through life we naturally look for the things, and seek the things, that meet our needs.

There is nothing at all wrong with that. But God also made us to find fulfillment through His abilities to supply our needs and satisfy our desires.[47] There would never be such a thing as division among us if all of us were living up to God's intentions for His Creation—if we were always satisfied with what God gives us and thankful for what He wants us to have.

If we remain a reflection of our Creator, we will always look to Him and trust Him to meet our needs. Our desires will be in line with His desires for us. And our focus will be on meeting the needs of others as His love continues to be reflected in us. There will be no room for division.

That's the way God meant it to be.

But the deceptive activity of our common enemy disrupted Adam and Eve's ability to live up to God's intention, and he is still doing everything he can to ruin forever *our* abilities to do it. And it should be clear that Satan is not the only one who can be

---

47 "And this same God who takes care of me will supply all your needs from his glorious riches, which have been given to us in Christ Jesus" (Philippians 4:19).

blamed for the division brought between God and man. Eve and her husband shared in the blame.

Yes, Eve fell prey to Satan's deception, but Adam and Eve also deceived themselves into deciding there was something to be gained by disobeying God. In effect, they deceived themselves into believing they could feed their own needs and desires with something outside the will of God. And they paid an awful price for it.

Today, we still pay a price for looking outside of God's supply and outside of God's will to satisfy our needs and desires. And as we do—when we go against God's plans for us and attempt to meet our own needs and desires instead of allowing Him to do it—it is no wonder that we find ourselves in conflict with others who are doing the same thing.

SATAN APPEALS TO IDENTITIES
AND EGOS TO DIVIDE US

Our identities and egos can get us into a lot of trouble. Satan knows he can cause havoc among us if he can find a way to use against us our need for affirmation and our all-too-strong tendency toward selfishness and self-absorption. He will do anything to leverage our identities and egos against us—to convince us that things like earthly fame and popularity are worth more than anything.

Our enemy wants to deceive us into believing we are better than others. He wants us to think our positions are more important than others. And he wants us to consider our own success more important than God's plan for us to contribute to the success of others.

The devil and his influences encourage our egos to lead us into developing prideful spirits. They appeal to our human nature to make us think we are more capable or more talented than others, so we *deserve* more respect or honor than the next person.

The enemy of our souls wants us to be consumed by who we are and how important we are to the world—and even to God. And he uses his influences to get us to believe personal satisfaction is more important than maintaining our relationships with others. He wants us to be consumed by who we are and how we're treated instead of focusing on how we treat others.

The division that comes from self-centered thoughts and actions is substantial and tragic. And our common enemy must find great joy in it. We need to determine in our hearts to disappoint him at every turn.

We are the ones who benefitted by Jesus refusing to fall for Satan's attempt to use Christ's identity and ego against Him. And others will benefit from us refusing to allow Satan to use our identities and egos against us. But to refuse the enemy's advances we must be wise to Satan's deceptions and yield our identities and egos to the control of the Holy Spirit.

SATAN APPEALS TO MANKIND'S DESIRES FOR THE WORLD'S TREASURES TO DIVIDE US

Of all the tactics used by the enemy to divide people, perhaps Satan's use of the world's treasures is one we can more easily recognize. And it is one that can not only be the most deceptive but also yield the most tragic results.

The appeal of what the world offers is strong on the flesh. And when God became man, our wonderful Lord found out just how strong it is. He experienced what it is like to live in relative poverty. And no doubt He experienced firsthand what it is like to look up from a pillow of stone to see the pleasures and power enjoyed by those living in luxury—those who possess the world's treasures.[48]

---

48 "But Jesus replied, 'Foxes have dens to live in, and birds have nests, but the Son of Man has no place even to lay his head'" (Luke 9:58).

But Satan didn't offer Jesus just a *share* of the world's treasures. Just think of the lifestyle, influence, and power that one would have if that person actually owned and ruled the entire world!

Jesus could have had it all, right then, instead of waiting for the Father to give it to him![49] But the cost to Jesus, to us, and to all of Creation would have been awful. And by yielding to Satan's offer He would have had to admit by that action that Satan had won.

But he didn't win. Satan didn't conquer either Jesus or God's plan. He didn't come between Jesus and His plan for our salvation. Our common enemy lost. He lost then. He is actually still losing now. And He will be the loser in eternity.

But unfortunately, Satan is still dangling the world's treasures before us. And all too many people are deceiving themselves into believing that having and enjoying the world's things is more important than having and enjoying the heavenly wealth God wants to give them.

More and more people today are being tempted to chase after the world's treasures and the pleasures they bring to the flesh. They desire and seek the world's treasures more than the treasures of heaven. They invest both too many resources and too much time enjoying or financing their pursuit of earthly things.

Today it may be considered old-fashioned to preach about how we can put things before God and make them our idols. But

---

49 While John the Baptist told his followers, "The Father loves his Son and has put everything into his hands" (John 3:35), that statement spoke of things far beyond the world's treasures they knew. And although Jesus in His deity—as God in the flesh—is already the creator and owner of the world and all that is in it (Psalm 24:1), His humanity made him subject to the power and rule of others who owned the earth's riches. Jesus now reigns with the Father, and they intervene in the affairs of men anytime they determine to do so, but it will not be until the Millennial Reign of Christ—when Jesus physically returns at a time of the Father's choosing (Mathew 24:36)—when He will receive the physical possession of the world and complete rule over it.

regardless of how the times have changed, man has not changed. And neither have the issues we deal with.

The things of the world that people spend their time and resources to possess—the things they are tempted to put before, or prioritize over, the things of God—can still become the idols they worship. And we need to take that seriously. Being deceived by the world into spending too much time and money on possessing what the world has to offer can divide our hearts from God.

What do we spend our money on? What do we spend our time doing? Has purchasing things to satisfy the flesh become more important than supporting the church or its worldwide mission? Has spending our time pursuing a favorite extracurricular activity become more important than time spent pursuing the heavenly treasures received by attending church, worshipping God, and being taught His Word?

To multitudes, Sundays have become the most popular day to attend games or participate in sports, to fish, golf, ride horses or ATVs, to go hiking, go camping, or run marathons instead of honoring the day as Christianity's Sabbath—the day belonging to the Lord and dedicated to rest and focused pursuit and worship of God. Don't let any of those things come between you and God.

None of those things I mentioned are wrong in their places, of course, but we must never allow them to become the things we follow instead of following God. When we put the pursuit of the world's treasures and pleasures above our pursuit of God, they become the focus of our worship. And that focus brings division. They divide our hearts from God, and eventually they will be used by the enemy to divide us from one another.

We are deceiving ourselves if we believe we can prioritize gaining the world's riches and pleasures over gaining heaven's riches without paying a spiritual price for it. We must not prioritize the things of the world over the things of God. And we must not be fooled into believing the treasures of the world will ever satisfy our desires for contentment and spiritual wholeness.

We must never allow Satan or his deceptive influences to get us to allow anything the world has to offer to get between us and God. And we must recognize that if we put anything between us and God, it will eventually result in getting between us and others.

It *will* divide us.

You and I share a common nature. We are subject to common temptations. And we share a common enemy whose tactics include using our common nature against us to divide us from God and one another.

The work of understanding and addressing this is crucial! We *must* successfully deal with these things, and God is here to help us do that. But we must yield ourselves to the Lord and allow His Holy Spirit to enlighten us, instruct us, and empower us for this work. And that is in God's plan for all of us.

God's Spirit dwells in Christians, and He wants to fill us all with wisdom and power. And the Holy Spirit is greater than the spirit who lives in the world.[50] It is God's will for us to overcome and defeat any attempt to divide us from God and others. The Holy Spirit will empower us to do it, but that will happen only when we determine to do so.

Satan remains a formidable opponent, and we must purposely recognize what he does and oppose him.

---

50 "But you belong to God, my dear children. You have already won a victory over those people, because the Spirit who lives in you is greater than the spirit who lives in the world" (1 John 4:4).

As Christians, we must battle against the enemy's attempts to divide us from God's will and from one another. Satan's goal is to use division to conquer us and interfere with God's will for our lives. He wants to conquer our lives, our families, and our nation. And if he gets his way, he will conquer our entire world.

We must keep Satan from dividing and conquering us. We must successfully battle against Satan's schemes, but to do that we must not only understand our enemy's tactics but also his limitations and God's preeminence over him.

And here is a key to that understanding:

Satan is a finite being. He was created by God but was cast out of heaven because of his pride and opposition to God and His plans. He is **not** equal to God. And unlike God, he is **not** omnipresent.

Yes, he is the prince and power of the air,[51] but as a finite being he can be in only one place at one time. While he personally used deception against Eve, and while he personally tempted Jesus in the wilderness, he cannot *personally* deceive or tempt each of the billions of people on earth at the same time.

But that does not keep him from using his influence to recruit and empower masses of people in the world to spread deception on his behalf. Satan is strategic and cunning. He can get one person with influence to buy into his deceptions and then use that person to spread deception and cause division around the world. We must recognize that and not deceive ourselves into falling into our enemy's traps.

God has ultimate power over Satan, and the Holy Spirit can empower every Christian—personally, worldwide, at the same time—to battle and gain the victory over Satan's deceptions. And

---

51 In the King James Version and several other Bible versions of Ephesians 2:2, Satan is called the *"prince and power of the air."* In the New Living Translation he is called *"the commander of the powers in the unseen world."*

He will do that if they yield themselves to God and follow Him into battle.

All of us, you and I, have a responsibility to be educated to both Satan's and the world's deceptive influences and attacks. Then we must walk in the power of the Holy Spirit, use what we know, and spread the word that it's time for us to wake up, refuse to be conquered, and expose all the deceptions that cause division.

Regardless of who is affected by division, it is heartbreaking and sad to see the pain and suffering it causes in the world. But sadder still is seeing how division so often affects the Church and its mission. It's painful to have to admit that the deception of the enemy works even within Christian circles.

The Church is not exempt from experiencing Satan's deceptions. And just because people have been born again and have joined a church doesn't mean they can never again allow themselves to be deceived—or never again deceive themselves—into accepting the devil's or the world's lies.

We should not be divided in addressing deception, temptation, and sin; but all too often we are. Even the church-world and entire denominations have become divided over critical issues—such as homosexuality, which is clearly and unequivocally addressed negatively in Scripture. As soon as someone stands and speaks to uphold the truth of God's word, another who claims to speak for God stands and says something to the effect of *"Did God really say . . . ?"* [52]

Does that sound familiar? It is deception.

---

52 Genesis 3:1.

What stark and clear deception Satan and his supporters have long been publishing in the world!

When it comes to God's Word, *YES*, God really said it! And we must not allow the enemy to separate us from God's truth. We must not be divided. Together, we must stand united in supporting and proclaiming what God said, what God is still saying, and what God is *doing* in the world today.

Accept truth, and reject deception along with the division it causes.

But when it comes to finding ourselves on one side of an issue or another (which is inevitable), when you find yourself caught up in division, make sure you are on God's side of every issue. His side is the right side, and it is the side that aligns itself with God's Word.

Those on God's side will not be conquered by deception and temptation. And they will not be divided from God's plan and purpose. When, like Jesus, they are tempted in a time of weakness and need, they will stand in Truth. And they will not just survive, but in the end they will prosper over those who constantly cause division and masquerade as holders of truth while they pull the wool over the eyes of others.

God is pulling the masks off of Satan and all others who foster division. And when their masquerade is over, they will be revealed as the truly conquered ones.

In that day the people will proclaim, "This is our God! We trusted in him, and he saved us! This is the LORD, in whom we trusted. Let us rejoice in the salvation he brings!" (Isaiah 25:9)

DISCUSSION QUESTIONS

1. In what ways has Satan used deception to cause division in your relationships?

2. What are the three ways Satan tempted Jesus?

3. Can you think of some ways Satan has used temptations like those in your own life?

4. What are some of the common things we are divided over today that we would never have imagined possible seventy years ago?

_____

_____

_____

_____

_____

_____

5. Why do you think it's more important today than ever before to find fellowship with a body of believers in a local church?

_____

_____

_____

_____

_____

_____

CHAPTER 9

THE DECEPTION OF CESSATION

AS I NEAR the end of this book I would be remiss if I didn't include a chapter about one of my very best friends—the Holy Spirit. I've mentioned Him in other places in the book, but this chapter is focused on and dedicated solely to Him.

The Holy Spirit is the very-important third person of the Trinity. And just as our knowledge of God would be incomplete without understanding the positions and purposes of God the Father and God the Son, understanding the position and purpose of God the Holy Spirit is just as important.

However, multitudes of Christians lack an adequate understanding of the importance of the Holy Spirit's place in the Godhead. So it's not surprising that many people can't accept the importance of the Holy Spirit's work today. They need to know that God's plans for us as individual believers, and the Church's work of fulfilling the Great Commission, cannot be accomplished without my wonderful friend.

Among the many things the Holy Spirit does in the world today, none is more important than His work of pointing people to Jesus. And His work of delivering God's Word and God's will to us has always been, and still is, absolutely critical. But there is more to know about Him.

For instance, just as the Father was seen and could be known through the physical manifestation of Jesus,[53] the Holy Spirit also was revealed and could be known through Jesus' life and ministry.

The Holy Spirit tangibly—visibly—descended upon Jesus in the form of a dove at Jesus' baptism.[54] It was a physical manifestation that was witnessed by others. And following that, the fullness and power of the Holy Spirit could constantly be seen in Jesus and through His ministry everywhere He went.[55]

When Jesus ministered to the crowds following His baptism, the Holy Spirit was clearly present in Jesus to provide authority and power to His words.[56] It was through the Holy Spirit that Jesus healed the sick, delivered the demon possessed, and performed other miracles.[57] And it's critical that we understand that.

---

53 "Philip said, 'Lord, show us the Father, and we will be satisfied.' Jesus replied, 'Have I been with you all this time, Philip, and yet you still don't know who I am? Anyone who has seen me has seen the Father! So why are you asking me to show him to you?'" (John 14:8-9).

54 "After his baptism, as Jesus came up out of the water, the heavens were opened, and he saw the Spirit of God descending like a dove and settling on him" (Matthew 3:16). "And the Holy Spirit, in bodily form, descended on him like a dove" (Luke 3:22a). See also Mark 1:10 and John 1:32.

55 "Then Jesus, full of the Holy Spirit, returned from the Jordan River. He was led by the Spirit in the wilderness" (Luke 4:1). "Then Jesus returned to Galilee, filled with the Holy Spirit's power" (Luke 4:14a).

56 "In my first book I told you, Theophilus, about everything Jesus began to do and teach until the day he was taken up to heaven after giving his chosen apostles further instructions through the Holy Spirit" (Acts 1:1-2).

57 "And you know that God anointed Jesus of Nazareth with the Holy Spirit and with power. Then Jesus went around doing good and healing all who were oppressed by the devil, for God was with him" (Acts 10:38).

Then, going beyond how the Holy Spirit fits into our understanding of the Godhead and the ministry of Jesus, we also need to know how the Holy Spirit works in and through the Church and the lives of individual Christians.

Everyone needs to know that after Jesus ascended back to Heaven after His resurrection, it was the same Holy Spirit who dwelled in and worked through Jesus who also descended upon believers to dwell in and work through them—just as Jesus promised. The Spirit descended once again to also give *their* words authority and empower *them* for ministry.[58]

After the believers were baptized in the Holy Spirit on the Day of Pentecost, they proclaimed the truth as they were empowered by the Spirit. The Holy Spirit worked through them like He did through Jesus. And their message was also confirmed with miraculous signs.[59]

And the Holy Spirit is still confirming the truths of the gospel message through signs and wonders today as He bestows spiritual gifts upon believers who accept them.

Drive a stake down by this: If Jesus needed and depended on the fullness of the Holy Spirit dwelling in Him to accomplish God's will, and if having the fullness and gifts of the Holy Spirit was necessary for believers in the early Church to accomplish *their* work, then we modern-day believers also need the Holy Spirit's power and miraculous gifts working through *us*.

But there are those who claim that is no longer necessary.

---

58 "But you will receive power when the Holy Spirit comes upon you. And you will be my witnesses, telling people about me everywhere—in Jerusalem, throughout Judea, in Samaria, and to the ends of the earth" (Acts 1:8). "After this prayer, the meeting place shook, and they were all filled with the Holy Spirit. Then they preached the word of God with boldness" (Acts 4:31).

59 Mark 16:20.

They have yielded their minds and hearts to the deceptive teaching of cessation. They believe the baptism—or infilling—of the Holy Spirit and the gifts of the Spirit are not needed by believers today like in biblical times. They believe there is no longer a reason for the spiritual gifts like tongues and interpretation of tongues, prophecy, healing, miracles, and others, to operate today.

People who believe in the teachings of *cessation*—that the supernatural gifts of the Holy Spirit are no longer necessary or needed to equip Christians for fulfilling God's plan for the Church (and by extension, His plan for the world)—are called *cessationists*.

In this chapter I deal with the deception behind the belief that so many of the important works of the Holy Spirit have ceased. And I call upon all my readers to reject the teachings of cessation and receive the fullness of the Holy Spirit along with any and all the spiritual gifts my dear friend wants to impart to them for successful Christian living and ministry.

The baptism of the Holy Spirit as an experience available to all Christians, and the impartation of the many miraculous gifts of my friend and advocate[60]—the Holy Spirit—have not ceased. He is still distributing His gifts to believers today, and they are still vital to the success of the Church.

I have a friend who tells everyone she comes in contact with about a certain product she has used. It worked wonders for her, and now she wants everyone to experience what it can do for them. She knows it works. She has experienced it firsthand, and her results were genuine. She believes in the product wholeheartedly.

---

60 "But when the Father sends the Advocate as my representative—that is, the Holy Spirit—he will teach you everything and will remind you of everything I have told you" (John 14:26).

She benefitted by using it, and now she wants everyone else to benefit from using it too.

That sentiment expresses exactly how I feel about the Holy Spirit and His gifts to the Church. I have experienced something that works, and I want to share it with the world.

Although the Holy Spirit is not a *product*, and He certainly is not something to be bought or sold, the amazing results of what He has done in my life, and what He is still doing, is undeniable. And I want everyone else to experience Him and His fullness in their lives too.

The Holy Spirit not only brought me *to* Jesus, He filled me with His power just as He did the believers on the Day of Pentecost. Then God spoke to me through the gentle wooing of the Holy Spirit to call me to ministry, and He gave me the boldness I needed to enable me to stand before others and declare Christ's message to the world.

The work of the Holy Spirit is progressive. It never ends. So after giving me boldness to minister the gospel, He began imparting to me various gifts of the Spirit for me to use in fulfilling the Great Commission. He continually takes me from one place in my relationship with Jesus to the next. And what the Holy Spirit has done for me, He will do for you.

Just as Peter's life was revolutionized when He was baptized in the Holy Spirit, my entire life also changed for the better when the Holy Spirit poured himself into me and brought me into a new life in the Spirit. And I want people to know that God wants to revolutionize their lives, too, by filling them to overflowing with the power of the Holy Spirit.

The Holy Spirit gives us the strength to stand strong and resist the enemy of our souls. And I believe that is the very reason Satan uses all the deception and influences he has to dissuade people from experiencing or desiring life in the Spirit. He'll do anything to convince believers that the baptism of the Holy Spirit and the gifts of the Spirit are no longer needed.

The enemy of our souls will use his influences both outside of churches and within churches—and even within whole denominations the world over—to make people skeptical and question the truth that the Holy Spirit is still doing the same thing today that He did in Peter's day to fulfill Christ's promise to believers.[61]

And as usual, behind those deceptive influences are the devil's lies!

The enemy is deceiving multitudes of Christians who desperately need the Holy Spirit in their lives. Lives are being wrecked. Churches are being wrecked. The world *is* a wreck. And we need the same wisdom, understanding, and power today that arrived in Jerusalem on the Day of Pentecost to meet and deal with the challenges before us.

Don't be deceived by anyone who claims the physical demonstrations and gifts of the Holy Spirit are no longer in operation. That is pure deception.

They are wrong!

---

61 "Once when he was eating with them [after His resurrection], he commanded them, 'Do not leave Jerusalem until the Father sends you the gift he promised, as I told you before. John baptized with water, but in just a few days you will be baptized with the Holy Spirit'" (Acts 1:4-5). "Peter replied, 'Each of you must repent of your sins and turn to God, and be baptized in the name of Jesus Christ for the forgiveness of your sins. Then you will receive the gift of the Holy Spirit. This promise is to you, to your children, and to those far away—all who have been called by the Lord our God'" (Acts 2:38-39). Based on context, the promised "gift" Peter spoke of is irrefutably the baptism of the Holy Spirit.

Most of what I have talked about in this book deals with issues related to salvation and the eternal consequences of yielding to spiritual deception. And no doubt, without letting the Holy Spirit do what He came to do in us, rejecting Him and His intentions could indeed impact our future and the future of others—even eternally.

But let me be clear that what I have to say in this chapter is not focused on salvation. I do not contend that Christians must experience the baptism of the Holy Spirit to be saved. And I do not contend that someone who has been baptized in the Holy Spirit and operates in the gifts of the Spirit is any more saved than a Christian who has not had those experiences.

No one can be more saved than *saved*.

By addressing the teaching of cessation I am stressing that if we reject the Holy Spirit's attempts to empower us like He empowered the early Church, we will miss out on what God wants to impart to us and do in and through us. (And of course that could certainly have consequences when it comes to evangelism and the salvation of others.)

And since the baptism of the Holy Spirit opens the door to other spiritual gifts that are important to the Church and her work, I want to stress that the value of the Pentecostal baptism should not be underrated. It is important for believers to desire and seek to be baptized in the Holy Spirit just like those believers on the Day of Pentecost.

As we begin to address beliefs in cessation, I want us to think about what spiritual gifts the believers of cessation want us to believe are no longer relevant to the ministry of the Church. Here is a passage of Scripture written by the Apostle Paul, in which he addressed those gifts:

There are different kinds of spiritual gifts, but the same Spirit is the source of them all. There are different kinds of service, but we serve the same Lord. God works in different ways, but it is the same God who does the work in all of us.

A spiritual gift is given to each of us so we can help each other. To one person the Spirit gives the ability to give wise advice; to another the same Spirit gives a message of special knowledge. The same Spirit gives great faith to another, and to someone else the one Spirit gives the gift of healing.

He gives one person the power to perform miracles, and another the ability to prophesy. He gives someone else the ability to discern whether a message is from the Spirit of God or from another spirit. Still another person is given the ability to speak in unknown languages, while another is given the ability to interpret what is being said.

It is the one and only Spirit who distributes all these gifts. He alone decides which gift each person should have.

(1 Corinthians 12:4-11)

Surely no one would contend that God no longer wants His followers equipped by the Holy Spirit with special abilities to *help* others. And surely even cessationists will admit the Holy Spirit gives to some believers special abilities to *discern* what is proper when dealing with spiritual matters and to provide people with *wise advice.*

After all, cessationists themselves must believe they have a God-given ability to *discern* spiritual matters since they are counseling the rest of us on what God thinks about today's relevancy of spiritual gifts. Surely they don't think giftings of the Holy Spirit are no longer needed in interpreting the Word of God and learning the intricacies of life in the Spirit. How ludicrous would that be?

So after considering this, it should become clear to us that people who believe the operation of any gifts of the Holy Spirit have ceased are being selective. There are only *certain gifts* they have problems with, not all the gifts. It's only the more demonstrative, physical, and miraculous gifts they want to deny.

Have you ever wondered why?

Let's take a look at some of the most commonly used arguments that cessationists make to convince people they're right.

MIRACULOUS GIFTS HAVE CEASED BECAUSE THAT WHICH IS PERFECT HAS COME

The following words of Paul are used to form one of the arguments in favor of cessation.

> *Love never fails. But whether there are prophecies, they will fail, whether there are tongues, they will cease; whether there is knowledge, it will vanish away. For we know in part and prophesy in part. But when that which is perfect has come, then that which is in part will be done away."* (1 Corinthians 13:8-10 NKJV)

These verses do mention that certain things associated with the gifts of the Holy Spirit will cease when that which is *perfect* has come. But many or most cessationists argue that perfection has already arrived. That is, the apostolic age—in which the more demonstrative gifts of the Holy Spirit were necessary—is over. The Canon of Scripture is complete. And the Church is established.

In effect, according to them, that is what Paul was talking about when it comes to the arrival of *that which is perfect.*

But that interpretation of Scripture falls flat. For Paul also said that *when that which is perfect has come*, knowledge will vanish away. Has knowledge vanished? Of course not. And do people still prophesy (speak on behalf of God)? Yes, of course. And cessationists themselves are in effect claiming to speak on God's behalf when they tell us certain gifts of the Holy Spirit are no longer in operation.

It is much more reasonable to see the time when perfection arrives as the day when Christ returns to rule. Or perhaps Paul was referring to when God makes the new heaven and earth.[62] But in any case, the perfection that Paul wrote about has yet to appear.

Paul was addressing believers in the Corinthian church. Some of them were guilty of taking pride in their spiritual gifts and misusing them. Paul wasn't trying to get them to stop receiving or using the gifts. He was trying to get them to maintain proper order and purpose in their use and stop prioritizing those gifts over love, which was the motivator their actions proved they were lacking.

MIRACULOUS GIFTS WERE ONLY FOR THE APOSTLES OF CHRIST

This argument—a prominent contention among those who began teaching cessation—maintains that the gifts of the Spirit were merely meant for the apostles, so the gifts of the Spirit ceased with the passing of the apostles. However, we can look

---

62 "Then I saw a new heaven and a new earth, for the old heaven and the old earth had disappeared. And the sea was also gone. And I saw the holy city, the new Jerusalem, coming down from God out of heaven like a bride beautifully dressed for her husband. I heard a loud shout from the throne, saying, 'Look, God's home is now among his people! He will live with them, and they will be his people. God himself will be with them'" (Revelation 21:1-3).

into the Word of God and easily see that the apostles were not the only ones used by the Holy Spirit to heal and work miracles.

When it comes to apostolic ministry within the early Church, the *apostles* were the disciples of Jesus (less Judas), Matthias (who was chosen by the disciples to replace Judas), and Paul.[63] Let's look at a few passages of Scripture where some notable things were done not by the apostles but by others.

Mark recorded that a man who was not even known to the disciples cast out a demon in the name of Jesus.

> *John said to Jesus, "Teacher, we saw someone using your name to cast out demons, but we told him to stop because he wasn't in our group."*
>
> *"Don't stop him!" Jesus said. "No one who performs a miracle in my name will soon be able to speak evil of me.* (Mark 9:38-39)

We know nothing more about the man. But we can assume he had fully accepted Jesus' ministry and considered himself a follower of the Messiah.

We also read in Acts that God instructed a certain believer, named Ananias, to go to where Paul was in Damascus and heal Paul's blindness. Ananias was not an apostle, and we have no information about any position of leadership he had in the Church.

> *The Lord said, "Go over to Straight Street, to the house of Judas. When you get there, ask for a man from Tarsus named Saul. He is praying to me right now. I have shown him a vision of a man named Ananias coming in and laying hands on him so he can see again."*
>
> *. . .*

---

63 1 Corinthians 1:1, 15:3-9.

So Ananias went and found Saul. He laid his hands on him and said, "Brother Saul, the Lord Jesus, who appeared to you on the road, has sent me so that you might regain your sight and be filled with the Holy Spirit." Instantly something like scales fell from Saul's eyes, and he regained his sight. Then he got up and was baptized. (Acts 9:11-18)

Then we read in the book of Luke what he recorded about Jesus one day sending out seventy-two disciples to heal and proclaim to people that the Kingdom of God was coming to them.

The Lord now chose seventy-two other disciples and sent them ahead in pairs to all the towns and places he planned to visit. (Luke 10:1)

Luke described them as seventy-two *other disciples.* The group did not contain the disciples who were to become known as the apostles of Christ. They were simply seventy-two others among all the followers of Jesus. Now, specifically note Jesus' final words to them after he gave them other instructions before they left.

Heal the sick, and tell them, "The Kingdom of God is near you now." (Luke 10:9)

Jesus told them to perform miracles of healing. Just from these few examples we can see the use of the Holy Spirit's miraculous gifts were never limited to the apostles alone, nor to those who were the converts or followers of the apostles.

The miraculous gifts of the Holy Spirit were actively used by believers before the "apostolic age' even began. The Holy Spirit's ministry has never been limited to such a small group of believers or time in history, and any such claim is just preposterous.

Normal everyday followers of Christ have long put their faith in His continuing power. They have received and used the gifts of the Spirit. They have prayed for the sick and performed miracles. And many people who cannot claim any special status of leadership in the Church are still being used by God today to minister to others through the Holy Spirit's gifts.

And for sure, Jesus wasn't just talking about the apostles or a small number of people in the early days of the Church when He said:

> *These miraculous signs will accompany* **those who believe**: *They will cast out demons in my name, and they will speak in new languages. They will be able to handle snakes with safety, and if they drink anything poisonous, it won't hurt them. They will be able to place their hands on the sick, and they will be healed."*
>
> (Mark 16:17-18 [emphasis mine])

MIRACULOUS GIFTS ARE ONLY NEEDED IN PLACES THAT ARE UNEVANGELIZED

One form of cessationist belief is called *Concentric Cessationism*.

Those who hold to this form of cessationism believe the miraculous gifts of the Spirit—including divine healing, prophecy, the working of miracles, tongues, and interpretation of tongues—have indeed ceased for well-established churches and denominations, but they still see a possibility they may appear during the work of evangelism where the Church has not yet been fully established.

I marvel at what they are thinking as I consider this particular belief. I wonder if the adherents of concentric cessationism have actually stopped to consider the full consequences of their claim. In truth, what they are saying is that they no longer need the miraculous gifts of the Spirit operating among them since their church or denomination is now up and running.

To me, people holding this view sure are proud of their churches and what they have accomplished! By extending their reasoning, it appears they think a church can become so well established and mature that it no longer needs the miraculous hand of *God the Holy Spirit* active among its members and in its ministry.

As I see it, they are being deceived into believing the *absence* of the gifts of the Holy Spirit is actually a sign of their church's health. That is much more than sad. It is alarming! And it is pure deception.

Dealing with this particular argument for cessation definitely causes me to wonder if cessationists are driven to form their beliefs because they need an excuse for no longer seeing God doing anything miraculous in their churches.

And is it any wonder that many churches and denominations that have long held such views of the baptism of the Holy Spirit and the gifts of the Spirit are on the decline today?

One of my favorite verses is found in Acts.

> *But you will receive power when the Holy Spirit comes upon you. And you will be my witnesses, telling people about me everywhere—in Jerusalem, throughout Judea, in Samaria, and to the ends of the earth.* (Acts 1:8)

Before saying those words to His disciples, Jesus had already told them to not leave Jerusalem until the Father sent to them His promised gift. Jesus commissioned them to take the good news to all the world, but in effect He was telling them to not even start doing that until they were baptized in the Holy Spirit.[64]

If Jesus felt it was so important for His followers in that day to be prepared like that for their work, is it not important that we are equally prepared for ours? We still desperately need the Holy Spirit's power. And we need all the giftings He can give us to continue answering the Great Commission—whether that takes us next door or around the world.

The disciples, along with many other believers, did as Jesus instructed them. They gathered together in Jerusalem in fellowship and prayer as they waited for the Father to send the Holy Spirit down upon them. And a few days later, the Father responded in a miraculous way.

On the day of Pentecost all the believers were meeting together in one place. Suddenly, there was a sound from heaven like the roaring of a mighty windstorm, and it filled the house where they were sitting. Then, what looked like flames or tongues of fire appeared and settled on each of them. And everyone present was filled with the Holy Spirit and began speaking in other languages, as the Holy Spirit gave them this ability. (Acts 2:1-4)

Multitudes of Jews from far and wide who lived in regions of the Roman Empire were gathered in Jerusalem to celebrate the feast of Pentecost, and it caused quite a stir among them when they witnessed the Holy Spirit baptize all those believers.

Part of those people who packed into Jerusalem marveled that some of the Spirit-filled believers were speaking in languages of their home countries when they knew they hadn't learned their languages.[65]

64 "Once when he was eating with them, he commanded them, "Do not leave Jerusalem until the Father sends you the gift he promised, as I told you before" (Acts 1:4).

65 Acts 2:7-11.

It was clear to others, though, that some of those believers spoke languages no one knew. And because of what they observed—those newly Spirit-filled people acted so strange and spoke such gibberish—they decided they were simply drunk.[66] But Peter—clearly a new man empowered by the Spirit—stood up before them and set them straight.

Then Peter stood up with the Eleven, raised his voice and addressed the crowd: "Fellow Jews and all of you who live in Jerusalem, let me explain this to you; listen carefully to what I say. These people are not drunk, as you suppose. It's only nine in the morning! No, this is what was spoken by the prophet Joel:

"'In the last days, God says, I will pour out my Spirit on all people. Your sons and daughters will prophesy, your young men will see visions, your old men will dream dreams. Even on my servants, both men and women, I will pour out my Spirit in those days, and they will prophesy.'" (Acts 2:14-18 NIV)

That was how the Church was born. It was birthed in the Pentecostal experience. It came into being in a demonstration of the power and gifts of the Holy Spirit. And there is not one word in the Bible that says anything about God's intentions for the empowerment and gifts of the Holy Spirit to ever decrease in the Church as long as God has work for believers to do.

Satan would have everyone believe the *Acts* of the Holy Spirit were meant to end, but they haven't. And wherever the Holy Spirit is welcomed by Christians, God will continue to empower them and their churches to prove cessationists wrong.

The deception of cessation is strong, especially among those who are unconsciously looking for an excuse for not allowing God's complete will to be done in their lives. But although

---

66 Acts 2:13.

this deception is welcomed by many people who don't want to acknowledge the truth for one reason or another, that is not always the case. And to me that makes the consequences of this deception even worse.

It is sad but true that a large number of well-meaning and sincere believers have unwittingly bought into some version of the belief of cessation because they simply don't know any better. They have not been instructed otherwise. They don't fully understand the Holy Spirit and the part He is supposed to play in their churches and in their lives.

They love Jesus. They want to follow Him. But for one reason or another they can't seem to look under the mask of deception to discover how they are being cheated. We need to help them do that. But we will not succeed without first welcoming the Holy Spirit to use us as He sees fit.

Don't let anyone, don't let the world, or even the devil himself deceive you and keep you back from pursuing all that God has for you in the Spirit. Seek the Holy Spirit's baptism. Approve and accept the gifts of the Holy Spirit.

Reject deception and let God do what He wants to do in your life.

DISCUSSION QUESTIONS

1. What is the most important work of the Holy Spirit, and why?

2. In what ways do you think Peter changed after the Holy Spirit descended on the Day of Pentecost?

_____

_____

_____

_____

_____

_____

3. Why do you think Satan tries to convince people that the Holy Spirit and His gifts are not for today?

_____

_____

_____

_____

_____

4. What types of doubt have you struggled with concerning the Holy Spirit and His work in the lives of believers today?

_____

_____

_____

_____

_____

5. Write Luke 11:11-13 in the space below. What do these verses tell us about trusting our Heavenly Father?

_____

_____

_____

_____

_____

_____

CHAPTER 10

THE COUNTERFEIT ANGEL OF LIGHT

I HAVE PURCHASED a lot of costume jewelry in my lifetime. And because of my taste in jewelry, some of that jewelry has been adorned with *cubic zirconia*.

Gemstones made of cubic zirconia—a manufactured, lab-produced mineral—began being mass produced in the mid-to-late 1970s. These gemstones often referred to as *imitation diamonds* quickly became popular and widely used in jewelry because of their low cost compared to diamonds. But that's not the only reason for their appeal. You see, cubic zirconia has another thing going for it.

Depending on the quality of the diamond it's compared to, a newly produced and faceted cubic zirconia gemstone will often appear more brilliant than a natural diamond. Unlike the most expensive diamonds, which can be graded as "perfect" or "flawless," the process of manufacturing cubic zirconia produces gems that are actually completely colorless—unlike all but the rarest diamonds—while containing no internal flaws. And they sparkle brightly.

But regardless of how good cubic zirconia jewelry looks when you first purchase it, it rarely stays that way. Cubic zirconia gemstones look a lot like diamonds, but they definitely are not. With enough time, their brilliance begins to fade. And depending on how they are cared for, they can soon lose their *sparkle*.

You see, cubic zirconia is not as hard and durable as diamond. Over time the sharp edges of cubic zirconia gemstones will show wear and become rounded—losing their sparkle. And unlike diamond, when cubic zirconia is polished it will allow certain microscopic scratch patterns to extend across multiple surfaces of the gem's facets. So frequent polishing of cubic zirconia can actually accelerate its loss of luster.

Genuine diamond is the hardest of any naturally occurring material on earth. And it has the highest thermal strength. That's why smaller and lower-quality diamond crystals are mined or produced synthetically in labs to be used in industry for cutting and polishing other materials. And it's the reason why when larger diamond crystals are cut into gemstones and polished, their shine and brilliance endures mistreatment.

Bottom line, diamonds can withstand incredible pressure, endure abuse, and retain their beauty longer than other gemstones. And those qualities combined with the rarity of larger gem-quality diamond crystals make diamonds so expensive.

In the jewelry business, cubic zirconia is known as a *diamond simulant*. It was developed to simulate diamond but be a cheaper alternative. Diamond simulants appeal to the human eye, but obviously, if you want something that will truly stand the test of time, you want to invest in the real thing.

As long as people understand what they're buying when they shop for jewelry, there is no problem with purchasing a cubic zirconia gemstone instead of a diamond. After all, a lot more people can afford purchasing a beautiful diamond simulant for fifty dollars than a diamond of similar size and beauty selling for thousands. But a real serious problem arises if someone is trying to sell a simulant claiming it is a diamond.

If you allow some person to sell to you what is supposed to be a $5,000 diamond in a genuine gold setting as a $2,000 bargain, and it turns out to be a $50 gem made of cubic zirconia mounted on top of a copper ring covered with thin gold plating, you've seriously been had. You've just purchased a counterfeit. You've lost a lot of money; some dishonest person made out like a bandit, so to speak; and you're left with a gumball-machine fake.

I don't know anyone who would want to be deceived into receiving a counterfeit of anything. Finding ourselves in possession of any kind of counterfeit product is frustrating. It makes us feel cheated and robbed. But there is something worse than owning a counterfeit piece of jewelry. Possessing a spiritual counterfeit is worse, and it can have eternal consequences.

It is far more important to make sure we are not fooled by a counterfeit when it comes to our spiritual lives and eternal future. And we must constantly be on guard against attempts by the enemy of our souls as he attempts to sell to us and to others a *bill of goods*.

Satan opposes God and God's plan for our lives. And in opposing God, the devil and his followers are constantly trying to take advantage of us and steal from us. He wants to cheat us, take from us anything God wants us to have—anything that will cause us to draw closer to God and prosper in His work—and replace it with a substitute.

Just as a dishonest person may try to sell an unsuspecting victim an imitation diamond ring as the real thing, our enemy also goes about marketing counterfeits. And he does it all the time. Among other things, he sells counterfeit knowledge, counterfeit wisdom, and counterfeit spirituality. In other words, he is always peddling counterfeit goods—including a counterfeit Christianity.

In His opposition to God and His ways, Satan is not only one who invents and promotes counterfeit things, I see him as the *king of counterfeit*. And in his never-ending attempt to promote substitutes for everything God has for us, he even tries to imitate God's work and appear to possess God's approval and authority.

The devil has always been envious of God. He wants what God has and more, and he does things to try to make his appeal to the world equal to or greater than God's. He is a thief, and he doesn't just steal from people; he does everything he can to steal from God too.

The devil wants to steal God's honor from people's hearts. He wants to steal from God people's worship and get them to worship at his own feet. He wants to steal God's followers and get them to follow him instead of God. And in his attempts to accomplish these things, he will actually stoop so low as to present himself as God's own emissary.

The Bible lets us know that Satan is so deceptive in his attempts to destroy God's kingdom that he will actually present himself as a follower of God and bearer of truth in the Lord's kingdom of *Light*.

> *Even Satan disguises himself as an angel of light.*
>
> (2 Corinthians 11:14b)

Satan will masquerade as God's representative sent to minister and carry the Lord's message, but he is nothing but a cheap counterfeit. He cannot come close to comparing himself and what he has to offer to our great and mighty God and what the Lord has to share with us, but he tries.

The Bible tells us about Satan and his deceptive nature. And the Scriptures expose not only Satan and his efforts but also the efforts of his followers. Below are several passages of Scripture that reveal things about Satan and his work. They speak to how he attempts to undermine God's work with his masquerade, and they show us what he really is behind the deceptive masks he wears.

THE TRINITY

To begin, here is a passage from the Bible that refers to the Trinity:

> *After his baptism, as Jesus came up out of the water, the heavens were opened and he saw the Spirit of God descending like a dove and settling on him. And a voice from heaven said, "This is my dearly loved Son, who brings me great joy."* (Matthew 3:16-17)

God—the Holy Trinity—consists of God the Father, God the Son, and God the Holy Spirit. Although there is only one God, we can see in a clear way from these verses in Matthew how God reveals himself and works through three distinct persons. Jesus (the Son) came up out of the water; the Holy Spirit descended upon Jesus like a dove in a clearly separate, physical manifestation; and the Father spoke in an audible voice from heaven—all at the same time.

It may be a mystery to us how one can be three and three can be one, but that is what the Bible says about the existence of God.

However, it is no mystery to Satan. He understands the reality and divine relationship within the trinity. And while dealing with Bible prophecy, many students of Scripture have talked about how Satan's envy will drive him to form his own unholy counterfeit trinity as he attempts to imitate God's work in the end times and use it to deceive the world. It is a trinity consisting of himself, the beast, and the false prophet.

But while many will be fooled by Satan's fakery, God will not allow it to stand.

Then the devil, who had deceived them, was thrown into the fiery lake of burning sulfur, joining the beast and the false prophet. There they will be tormented day and night forever and ever.

(Revelation 20:10)

God will not allow himself or His works to be imitated without answering it. He will not share either His position or His glory with Satan. In the coming Day of Judgment, Jesus will put an end to Satan's schemes. And He will banish the trinity of deception to the lake of fire forever.

THE CHILDREN

Those who have put their trust in God and have accepted Jesus Christ as their Savior—those who have accepted His Sacrifice as the atonement for their sins—are the sons and daughters of God. They have become known as God's children, and they are dearly loved by Him.

> *But to all who believed him and accepted him, he gave the right to become children of God.* (John 1:12)

But Satan also has children. And just as God's children reflect the nature of God, Satan's children reflect his. When addressing the people who were plotting to kill Him, Jesus said to them:

> *For you are the children of your father the devil, and you love to do the evil things he does. He was a murderer from the beginning. He has always hated the truth, because there is no truth in him. When he lies, it is consistent with his character; for he is a liar and the father of lies.* (John 8:44)

Satan is a murderer and the father of lies, and his children are deadly and liars like him. And the devil uses his children to promote his own agenda. He presents himself, and his children present themselves, as having the truth to share with the world. But they lie, and he and all his lying children will one day come to judgment.

> *But when the Son of Man comes in his glory, and all the angels with him, then he will sit upon his glorious throne. All the nations will be gathered in his presence, and he will separate the people as a shepherd separates the sheep from the goats. He will place the sheep at his right hand and the goats at his left.* (Matthew 25:31-33)

Then the King will turn to those on the left and say, "Away with you, you cursed ones, into the eternal fire prepared for the devil and his demons." (Matthew 25:41)

God truly loves His children. He cares for them, and they will enjoy a wonderful future that He has planned for them. But while Satan may appear to love his followers, he does not. Even his care for them is counterfeit. He actually hates them and covers up his true intention of eventually taking them to the lake of fire with him.[67]

THE APOSTLES

The initial disciples of Christ were twelve men whom Jesus chose to join Him in His work. Jesus appointed them to spread and confirm His message with signs and wonders.

Jesus called his twelve disciples together and gave them authority to cast out evil spirits and to heal every kind of disease and illness. (Matthew 10:1)

Those disciples later became known as the *apostles* of Christ—special representatives and leaders chosen by God. They were anointed by the Holy Spirit to continue the Lord's work on earth

---

67 "And I saw a great white throne and the one sitting on it. The earth and sky fled from his presence, but they found no place to hide. I saw the dead, both great and small, standing before God's throne. And the books were opened, including the Book of Life. And the dead were judged according to what they had done, as recorded in the books. The sea gave up its dead, and death and the grave gave up their dead. And all were judged according to their deeds. Then death and the grave were thrown into the lake of fire. This lake of fire is the second death. And anyone whose name was not found recorded in the Book of Life was thrown into the lake of fire" (Revelation 20:11-15).

in His absence.[68] Years later, God chose Saul of Tarsus (who became best known by the Greek form of his name, Paul) to also be an apostle of Christ.[69]

Satan also recruits people to follow and represent him as leaders to carry out his deceptive work, and he influences some of them to join him in such deceitfulness that they become counterfeit apostles of Christ. He places them among true believers and uses them to imitate and undermine Christ's work from within. Paul wrote to the Corinthians about them.

These people are false apostles. They are deceitful workers who disguise themselves as apostles of Christ. But I am not surprised! Even Satan disguises himself as an angel of light.

(2 Corinthians 11:13-14)

As leaders among the children of the father of lies, such false apostles participate in the devil's masquerade as they pull people into Satan's deception through their increased influence and control.

THE TWO MARKS

While persecuted and living in exile toward the end of his life, the Apostle John wrote what is now known as the book of Revelation to reveal what God showed to him about what was to come in the last days. He spoke of two marks. One mark was the seal of God.

---

68 "Here are the names of the twelve apostles: first, Simon (also called Peter), then Andrew (Peter's brother), James (son of Zebedee), John (James's brother), Philip, Bartholomew, Thomas, Matthew (the tax collector), James (son of Alphaeus), Thaddaeus, Simon (the zealot), Judas Iscariot (who later betrayed him)" (Matthew 10:2-10). Following the death of Judas, Mathias was chosen by the eleven remaining disciples to replace Judas and join them as one of the twelve. See Acts 1:15-26.

69 Galatians 1:1.

John wrote about how God will mark His own with a seal of His ownership on their foreheads.

> *And I saw another angel coming up from the east, carrying the seal of the living God. And he shouted to those four angels, who had been given power to harm land and sea, "Wait! Don't harm the land or the sea or the trees until we have placed the seal of God on the foreheads of his servants.* (Revelation 7:2-3)

The Lord knows who His children are, and He will place His very own seal upon them to confirm it. And when it comes to protecting His children, the possession of God's seal upon them will save His children from wrath.

> *Then the fifth angel blew his trumpet, and I saw a star that had fallen to earth from the sky, and he was given the key to the shaft of the bottomless pit. When he opened it, smoke poured out as though from a huge furnace, and the sunlight and air turned dark from the smoke. Then locusts came from the smoke and descended on the earth, and they were given power to sting like scorpions.* ***They were told not to harm the grass or plants or trees, but only the people who did not have the seal of God on their foreheads.*** (Revelation 9:1-4 [emphasis mine])

Then John wrote of the second mark, and it is a mark no one should desire.

Just as God will mark those who belong to Him in order to protect them—to provide them security from experiencing God's wrath—Satan also is planning in the future to use a mark to offer security to people, but that mark will be revealed as counterfeit. It will provide them no lasting security.

Satan's mark will in effect become a seal of Satan's rule over his followers—those who have rejected Christ—and instead of providing security to them it will end up providing them nothing but trouble.

We refer to this second mark as the *mark of the beast*.

As recorded in the thirteenth chapter of Revelation, John foretold the appearance of *the beast*. The beast is most often interpreted to be the antichrist. Following the introduction of the beast into his narrative, John wrote of a *second beast* who will appear. And the second beast will represent and exercise the authority of the first beast.[70]

The second beast is commonly known as *the false prophet*. Among the deeds of the false prophet, which include performing signs and causing people to worship the first beast, John told of the mark that the false prophet will cause to be set upon all people who follow and worship the beast.

> *He required everyone—small and great, rich and poor, free and slave—to be given a mark on the right hand or on the forehead. And no one could buy or sell anything without that mark, which was either the name of the beast or the number representing his name.* (Revelation 13:16-17)

The first mark John wrote about—the seal of God—will be used in the last days in a special way to protect God's children from pain and sorrow.[71] That first mark is in effect a seal of life. But the second mark—Satan's counterfeit—will be a seal of destruction.

> *Then a third angel followed them, shouting, "Anyone who worships the beast and his statue or who accepts his mark on the*

---

70 Revelation 13:11-12.

71 John wrote of 144,000 being sealed (see Revelation 7:4-8). Some have believed this actually refers to only Jews living in Israel. But others contend that number is symbolic of all faithful believers in both the Old Testament and New Testament days by using the numeric symbolism that exists in Scripture. For a fuller, thoughtful, and detailed explanation of this, I recommend reading subsections, Hold Back the Wind and The 144 Thousand, pages 94-98 of *Approaching Judgment: the Path to Armageddon*, by David A. Womack, published by Bridge-Logos, 2016—[Editor].

> *forehead or on the hand must drink the wine of God's anger. It has*
> *been poured full strength into God's cup of wrath. And they will be*
> *tormented with fire and burning sulfur in the presence of the holy*
> *angels and the Lamb. The smoke of their torment will rise forever*
> *and ever, and they will have no relief day or night, for they have*
> *worshiped the beast and his statue and have accepted the mark of*
> *his name."*   (Revelation 14:9-11)

A day of reckoning is coming for the world. When all the masks are removed on the Day of Judgment, on that very day, the world will know the masquerade is over.

As Jesus revealed to John, the day is coming when Satan's deceptive work, and that of his followers, will indeed come to an end. But sadly, their deceptions continue today, and many are being fooled into believing the devil's lies.

Even many who have lived their entire lives following Christ are now listening to and allowing themselves to be tempted by the deceptions in false teachings. And by doing so they are giving their ears to a counterfeit gospel, becoming complacent, and living in danger of falling away.[72]

More and more people are accepting the devil's deceptions and living in darkness. But while that is happening we are also seeing millions come to Christ around the world. While the devil's masquerade as an angel of light continues as he promotes all forms of deception, God also continues to reveal His Light and confirm the Truth that will always dispel the darkness.

There is a small town called Rjukon in Norway. It sits in a deep, narrow valley surrounded by huge mountains. Because of

---

72 2 Thessalonians 2:1-3 (KJV).

its location, the mountains block the sun for six months of every year, making Rjukon one of the darkest towns in the world. For half of the year the town is covered by shade, with its inhabitants seeing no sunlight.

Eventually, one man decided to do something about it. He came up with a plan to design a system of large sun-tracking mirrors to be placed on top of one of the mountains with the intention of reflecting sunlight down into the town.

Some of the townspeople thought it was a great idea. Others, though, thought he was crazy and tried their best to stop his plans. They just couldn't imagine spending the kind of money it would take to install giant mirrors on the mountaintop.

Despite all the pushback from the naysayers, though, the man's plan was adopted, and in 2013 the project was completed. A great ceremony was held in the town square, and the mirrors were finally unveiled.

It worked! The town of Rjukon experienced sunlight in the winter for the very first time. The mirrors reflected the light of the sun down into the town square.[73]

The reflected sunlight only shines on an area covering about 6,400 square feet. That's roughly the size of one-tenth of a football field. That is not a very big area. But still, people drive for several hours to visit the town and stand in the light for just a few minutes.

The people have a desire to see the light and feel the warmth of the sun on their skin. And the economy has benefited from all the tourism the project has generated. Now this small town thrives. A whole town has been changed for the better because of the light that now shines there throughout the long, dark winter months—in the midst of darkness.

---

73 https://www.theguardian.com/world/2013/nov/06/rjukan-sun-norway-town-mirrors

Despite the attempts of some of the people to prevent the project from taking place, others stood together and fought to allow sunlight to pour into their small town. And like the mirrors on that mountain reflecting the light of the sun onto the town of Rjukon, we stand together to reflect the light of Christ into the world—into spiritual darkness.

Satan masquerades as an angel of light, while he has nothing but darkness to offer. But he continues to promote his deception and recruit others to join him in selling to the world his counterfeit goods. And many people today walk in darkness because they have been fooled into accepting them.

As we continue our march toward the times John wrote about, I don't doubt that the days will become spiritually darker and darker. It will get so dark that people will eventually be willing to accept the counterfeit miracles performed by the false prophet to lure them away from Christ.[74]

But Jesus said we, His children, are the *light of the world*, and like a city on a hilltop we cannot be hidden.[75] We know that any light we are—and have to share—is the Lord's light.[76] But we also

---

74 2 Thessalonians 2:8-10.

75 Matthew 5:14.

76 Christ's followers can be called the *light of the world* only because they reflect the person, character, and mission of Jesus. Before we could become the light of the world, Jesus first had to come to be the true light of origin—the light we reflect—or we would have nothing to share with those living in darkness. We would have nothing to reflect into the world in which they live without Christ first shining His light on us. "Jesus spoke to the people once more and said, 'I am the light of the world. If you follow me, you won't have to walk in darkness, because you will have the light that leads to life'" (John 8:12).

know that when we reflect that light and allow it to shine into the darkness, the darkness is dispelled.

As the days become more dark and evil, we must strive to shine brighter. Just as a diamond endures and retains its brilliance to glitter in the sun long after it is formed, and just as the mirrors on the mountain above Rjukon reflect the sunlight down on the town in the winter, we must endure and continue to reflect the *Light of the SON.*

If we cling to the Word of God, pray, and intercede for our nation and world, I believe our light will grow brighter in these dark times and those to come. And as we stand together—as we pursue the truth of God and reject all counterfeits—I believe we will make a difference.

And we can do that because, like a genuine diamond, *the Light*—Jesus Christ—will endure long after Satan's masquerade has ended. That *Light* can never be extinguished, and the darkness— Satan's deceptions—cannot prevail against *Him.*

> *The Word gave life to everything that was created, and his life brought light to everyone. The light shines in the darkness, and the darkness can never extinguish it.*   (John 1:4-5)

DISCUSSION QUESTIONS

1. Can you think of other ways Satan has tried to imitate God and His power?

_____

_____

_____

_____

_____

_____

2. Write 1 Timothy 6:15-16 in the space below. What do you see in this verse that could explain why Satan masquerades as an angel of light?

_____

_____

_____

_____

_____

3. It has been said that imitation is the best form of flattery. However, in many cases it stems from foolish comparison, jealousy, and coveting what belongs to others. We want to live our lives in such a way that others, especially our children, want to emulate the good we are or have done. But have you had anyone in your life who tried to imitate you in a way you felt was negative? Did you find it flattering, or did you feel like the individual wanted to be you?

_____

_____

_____

_____

_____

4. A. W. Milne labored as a missionary in a section of New Guinea where there were many cannibals. There, he died preaching the gospel of Jesus Christ. His converts, some of whom were former cannibals, asked permission to place a marker on his grave, on which they inscribed: "Here lie the remains of A.W. Milne. When he came to us there was no light. When he

died there was no darkness." I love that epitaph. If you were to witness your own epitaph, how would you hope it would read? What kind of legacy do you hope to leave?

_____

_____

_____

_____

_____

_____

5. List a couple of ways we can bring light to the darkness in the world in which we live.

_____

_____

_____

_____

_____

_____

EPILOGUE

· ·

DECEPTION RULES IN far too many places here on earth. It rules in far too many hearts, far too many homes, far too many churches, and far too many nations. But no deception dwells in heaven. With that in mind, the Lord's Prayer has a special application to me as we close this book in prayer.

> *Our Father in heaven,*
> *Hallowed be Your name.*
> ***Your kingdom come.***
> ***Your will be done***
> ***On earth as it is in heaven.***
> *Give us this day our daily bread.*
> *And forgive us our debts,*
> *As we forgive our debtors.*
> ***And do not lead us into temptation,***
> ***But deliver us from the evil one.***
> ***For Yours is the kingdom and the power and the glory forever.***
> *Amen* [77]

May it be on earth like it is in heaven. May our lives be delivered from the evil one and freed from all his deceptions just as heaven is free of them.

That is our plea as we call out to God right now. Just as Truth reigns in heaven, may Truth also reign here and displace all the lies and deceptions that so often run rampant among us. May Truth live among us to overcome and destroy all the

---

77 Matthew 6:9-13 (NKJV).

intentions of the enemy of our souls and the plans of others who oppose God.

It is going to happen. The day is coming. But knowing that is not good enough for true and faithful believers. Yes, their minds are on future hope, but they are active today and every day not only praying for that day to come but also speaking truth to confront falsehood and deception wherever it exists.

They are bringing people to Jesus, teaching them, and discipling them to be strong in the faith and deeply rooted in the gospel of Jesus Christ. They are sharing the Words of Life with others and preparing hearts and minds for overcoming deception as they joyfully anticipate the return of our Lord and Savior.

If you don't know for certain that you are prepared to meet Christ when He returns, I invite you to pray a simple prayer with me and mean it from deep within your own heart.

Dear Father in heaven,

Thank you for revealing your truth to me. I am convinced you love me and want to deliver me from all deception. I believe Jesus died for me so I might have life. I accept His sacrifice for my sins. And I want to live for you and trust your Holy Spirit to lead me for the rest of my life.

I want to live my life as your child and reflect your nature and light as a testimony to others of your love and your desire to also deliver them from deception, save them from sin, and revolutionize their lives for your glory.

Share with me your wisdom so I will always do what is pleasing in your sight. And fill me with the power of your Holy Spirit so I will walk boldly in your light as you lead me down the path in life you have for me.

I love you, and I commit myself to you in the name of Jesus.

BEAUTY FROM ASHES
Donna Sparks

In a transparent and powerful manner, the author reveals how the Lord took her from the ashes of a life devastated by failed relationships and destructive behavior to bring her into a beautiful and powerful relationship with Him. The author encourages others to allow the Lord to do the same for them.

Donna Sparks is an Assemblies of God evangelist who travels widely to speak at women's conferences and retreats. She lives in Tennessee.

www.story-of-grace.com

www.facebook.com/
donnasparksministries/

www.facebook.com/
AuthorDonnaSparks/

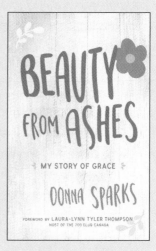

ISBN: 978-1-61036-252-8

NO LIMITS
Donna Sparks

The naysayers of the world want to convince us that the days of God working miracles have passed. But in *No Limits: Embracing the Miraculous*, Donna Sparks uses contemporary testimonies of powerful miracles released into the lives of believers and non-believers alike to show God has not changed. He has worked miracles in the past, and there are no limits on His ability to work miracles today!

Donna Sparks is an Assemblies of God evangelist who travels widely to speak at women's conferences and retreats. She lives in Tennessee.

www.story-of-grace.com

www.facebook.com/
donnasparksministries/

www.facebook.com/
AuthorDonnaSparks/

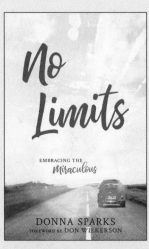

ISBN: 978-1-61036-402-7

SWING WIDE
Keri Cardinale

After years of believing she was "born this way," Keri hit a wall when faced with the decision to marry a woman. With a slight hesitation in her heart and a faint memory of the love she once had for Jesus, Keri chose to walk away from the life she knew and gave God the chance to show her who she was made to be.

Swing Wide is a love story, not a gay story.

It's a story about experiencing the greatest love of all—the love that knows no bounds.

kericardinale.com

ISBN: 978-1-61036-400-3